SCHOLASTIC

Essential English

Course Book

Level 5

Page 116 constitutes an extension of the copyright page.

Published by Scholastic India Pvt. Ltd.
A subsidiary of Scholastic Inc., New York, 10012 (USA).
Publishers since 1920, with international operations in Canada, Australia, New Zealand, the United Kingdom, Mexico, India, Argentina, and Hong Kong.

For information regarding permission, write to:
Scholastic India Pvt. Ltd.
A-27, Ground Floor, Bharti Sigma Centre
Infocity-1, Sector 34, Gurgaon (Haryana) - 122001
Email: education@scholastic.co.in

Typeset at Digital Expressions

First edition: 2008
Reprinted: 2009 (twice), 2011, 2012, 2013, 2014, 2017, 2024, 2026

ISBN: 978-81-8477-143-5

Printed at : Saurabh Printers Pvt. Ltd.

Contents

S. No.	Language Development				
	Lesson	Reading Comprehension	Vocabulary	Grammar	Spelling & Punctuation
1	The Cemetery of Chateau d'If (Story)	Drawing inferences and comprehending details	Masculine, feminine and neuter words/ Opposites	Singular and plural nouns/Concrete and abstract nouns	Punctuation
2	Yudhishtir the Just (Story)	Drawing inferences and comprehending details	Collective nouns/Compound nouns	Types of nouns	Syllables
3	What's Eating You? (Story)	Drawing inferences and comprehending details	Names of phobias/Identifying the odd word	Making sentences/Types of sentences	Spelling rules
4	Trees (Poem)	Understanding the poem	Antonyms/Using accept and except	Possessive nouns/Countable and uncountable nouns	Suffixes 'ous' and 'able'
5	After Twenty Years (Play)	Drawing inferences and comprehending details	Synonyms/Using affect and effect	Phrases/Interrogative sentences	Using commas
6	I'm Only a Child (Speech)	Drawing inferences and comprehending details	Past and present tense	Doing verbs/Helping verbs/Changing tenses	Reading and pronouncing 'sc' and 'sk' words
7	Don't Do As I Say (Story)	Drawing inferences and comprehending details	Adverbs/Contractions	Tenses/Positive and negative sentences	Spelling rules
8	He Wishes for the Cloths of Heaven (Poem)	Understanding the poem	Participles	Tenses	Spelling rules
9	All About Stars (Non-fiction)	Drawing inferences and comprehending details	Names of food/Similes	Parts of a sentence/Transitive and intransitive verbs	Apostrophes
10	In the Fog (Story)	Drawing inferences and comprehending details	Homophones/ Homographs	Subject and predicate/Phrases	Reading and pronouncing words that end in 'ible' and 'able'
11	The Boy Who Could Not Finish A (Story)	Drawing inferences and comprehending details	Similes/Words that go together	Comparative adjectives/Number adjectives	Question tags/ Homophones
12	Three Characters (Poem)	Understanding the poem	Prefixes	Interrogative pronouns and adjectives/ Prepositions	Reading and pronouncing 'tion and 'sion' words
13	Bani Chatterji and the Burden of Expectation (Story)	Drawing inferences and comprehending details	Idioms/Words and their meanings	Possessive pronouns and adjectives/ Conjunctions	Quotation marks
14	Alexander Graham Bell (Biography)	Drawing inferences and comprehending details	Suffixes	Adverbs (time, place, manner, frequency)	Anagrams
15	Wilderness (Story)	Drawing inferences and comprehending details	Phrases	Clauses	Direct and indirect speech
16	Word Balloon (Poem)	Understanding the poem	Choosing the correct word	Personal and possessive pronouns/ Relative pronouns/ Reflexive pronouns	Editing text

Communication Skills			Social Skills	Fun T ime	
Writing	Listening	Speaking	Everyday English	Activity	Read More
Writing a story	Identifying true and false sentences	Asking and answering questions		Word game	✓
Putting a story in sequence	Identifying odd words	Class discussion		Dictionary game	✓
Writing a paragraph	Identifying based on descriptions	Speaking about your dream vacation	Planning an excursion	Shrinking words	✓
Writing a story from the given beginning	Answering a question	Discussing the poem		Photo report: Your favourite tree	
Writing a play	Listening for silent letters	Discussion of memories	Booking a table at a restaurant	Word change	✓
Writing a formal letter	Answering questions	Making a speech		Word origins	
Writing an informal letter	Answering a riddle	Asking and guessing riddles		Mystery word	✓
		Reciting a poem			
Writing a summary	Listening to role play	Class discussion	At the airline check-in counter	Man words	✓
Making a poster	Listening to answer	Talking about a book		Crossword	✓
Describing a place	Identifying homophones	Discussing cuisines	At the shoe shop	Proverbs	✓
Writing a poem					
Writing a blog	Identifying idioms	Debating		Group of three	
Taking a telephone message	Identifying household objects	Conversing using 'could I' and 'should I'	Making a telephone complaint	Crossword	✓
Writing a book review	Listening to answer questions	Speaking about experiences		Wil words	✓
Favourite words					

Thank You!

The *Essential English* books were sent out to approximately eighty schools across the country for primary school principals, departmental heads and teachers to give their feedback on the contents.

The publishers would like to thank all those who took the time out of their busy schedules to go through the books and make many valuable suggestions, which have been duly incorporated.

Abha Arora, Delhi Public School, Chandigarh
Alka Patankar, Sanskriti School, New Delhi
Angela Ghosh, St James' School, Kolkata
Anjali, Yadavindra Public School, Patiala
Anjum Rahim, Delhi Public School, Raipur
Arpita Anand, Navy Children's School, New Delhi
Ch. Naveena Kumari, BSD DAV Public School, Hyderabad
Chandana, Lancer's Convent, New Delhi
Garima Wadhwa, Bal Bharati Public School, New Delhi
Harmeen Kaur, Delhi Public School, Chandigarh
Harmeet Kaur, St Mark's Senior Secondary Public School, New Delhi
Intu Ghuman, Yadavindra Public School, Patiala
Iyer Rama Chandrashekar, Sunshine School, Rajkot
Kanika Kumar, Lancer's Convent, New Delhi
Lakshmi Satish, Head Start Learning Centre, Chennai
Lakshmi Subramanian, consultant, Hyderabad
Maneesha Gupta, Sanskriti School, New Delhi
Manju Gupta, Pallavi Model School, Hyderabad
Matthew Panamkat, Doon Public School, New Delhi
Mitali Ghosh, Sunshine School, Rajkot
Monica Keswani, Bal Bharati Public School, New Delhi
N. Purohit, Sunshine School, Rajkot
N.R. Sailaja, BSD DAV Public School, Hyderabad
Nandita Majumdar, BSD DAV Public School, Hyderabad
Neeru Bhaskar, Delhi Public School, Kanpur
Nirmal Muku, Vidya Niketan Senior Secondary School, New Delhi
Padma Singh, Pallavi Model School, Hyderabad
Pamela Banerjee, Delhi Public School, Kanpur
Peter Lauenstein Denzongpa, Taktse International School, Sikkim
Pooja Khurana, Lancer's Convent, New Delhi
Priti Kathpalia, Sanskriti School, New Delhi
Priyanka Khare, Delhi Public School, Raipur
Priyanka, Lancer's Convent, New Delhi
R. Sumathy, Delhi Public School, Raipur
Ravneet Walia, Yadavindra Public School, Patiala
Reena Nagpal, Yadavindra Public School, Patiala
Renu Vashishta, Maharana Mewar Vidya Mandir, Udaipur
Renuka, Lancer's Convent, New Delhi
Reshma Thapa, Taktse International School, Sikkim
Rima Nijh, Delhi Public School, Chandigarh
Rinku Bhowmick, Navy Children's School, New Delhi
Ritika Sharma, Navy Children's School, New Delhi
Roma Gupta, Navy Children's School, New Delhi
Rubina Majid, school consultant, Hyderabad
Ruchi Verma, Delhi Public School, Chandigarh
S. Purushutham, Delhi Public School, Raipur
S. Sivasankari, Delhi Public School, Raipur
S.K. Sodhi, BSD DAV Public School, Hyderabad
Sabira A. Dal, Sunshine School, Rajkot
Sangeeta Chaudhury, The Gurukul, Panchkula
Sangeeta Sharma, Delhi Public School, Chandigarh
Sangita Malik, Yadavindra Public School, Patiala
Sarika Kapoor, Lancer's Convent, New Delhi
Sarita, Lancer's Convent, New Delhi
Savithri Radhakrishnan, Head Start Learning Centre, Chennai
Seema Pathak, Vidya Niketan, New Delhi
Sharon Galstaun, St Karen's Nursery School, Patna
Shylaja R., AMM Matriculation Higher Secondary School, Chennai
Sister Philomena, Holy Cross English Primary School, Aurangabad
Sonia Dheer, The Gurukul, Panchkula
Sonisha, Lancer's Convent, New Delhi
Sudha Suresh, Vidya Mandir Senior Secondary School, Chennai
Suman Lata Pradhan, Taktse International School, Sikkim
T. Sharada, Lancer's Convent, New Delhi
T.S.S. Reddy, consultant, Hyderabad
Teena Agarwal, Bal Bharati Public School, New Delhi
The teachers of G.D. Goenka Public School, New Delhi
The teachers of St Mark's Senior Secondary Public School, New Delhi
V. Subhashini, Subhaniketan, Kakinada
Vaishali and Manisha Gadekar, Kids Edutainment Centre, Mumbai
Varnika, Lancer's Convent, New Delhi
Veena S. Kumar, Navy Children's School, New Delhi
Vishali Kapoor, Delhi Public School, Kanpur
Y. Cabral, Methodist High School, Kanpur

In addition to the people listed above, there were many teachers who did not want their help to be publicly acknowledged. In deference to their wishes, we have not included their names, but we would once again like to acknowledge their valuable help.

Introduction

Essential English, a series of innovative activity-based course books, is a valuable learning tool. The books use the communicative approach to help students improve their written and verbal skills and appreciate how the various elements of English are used to convey meaning. The approach follows the current NCERT curriculum and pedagogical principles.

In addition, the books aim to foster a love of literature and reading in children. This has been done by a careful selection of age-appropriate literary pieces by well-known Indian and international authors, designed to stimulate children's imagination and inculcate a life-long interest in reading.

The books have been created by a panel of eminent authors, school and college teachers, and experienced children's publishers, and vetted by school teachers and principals from different parts of India.

The *Essential English* series has been designed to cover the essential skills of the language:

Language development:

- Reading comprehension
- Vocabulary
- Grammar
- Spelling and punctuation

Communication skills:

- Writing
- Listening
- Speaking

Social and other skills:

- Everyday English
- Activity
- Read More (for Classes IV and V)

Some of the unique features of this series are:

The selection of texts

You will notice from the table of contents that the books contain an interesting mix of short stories by distinguished authors, extracts from well-known novels, poems, plays, speeches, biographies and non-fiction articles on varied subjects. The texts selected are both classic and contemporary so that students are introduced to different kinds of writing. Students will enjoy reading a wide variety of stories and articles that are humorous, exciting and informative.

Introduction to well-loved authors

The authors for most of the pieces are well-known Indian or international authors, who write for the appropriate age group. We believe that reading the finest writing available in a range of different styles will aid children to learn the language better.

Illustrations in diverse styles

Each text is illustrated in a style appropriate to its contents with paintings, pencil sketches, collages or photographs to encourage the child's aesthetic appreciation of different kinds of art.

Encouragement to understand and analyse

The reading comprehension sections are a combination of inference questions designed to make the child read the text closely, and critical response questions that encourage the child to think and analyse character, situation, moral values and ideas. The poems are followed by questions to make the child appreciate poetry and understand the different nuances of the poem.

Learning through fun

The activities include word puzzles, riddles and other fun ways of finding answers and are tools for improving comprehension. Finding the main idea, paying attention to details, drawing conclusions and following directions are just some of the skills included.

Learning through practice

Each lesson contains challenging vocabulary and grammar sections. The grammar exercises are contextualised to contribute meaningfully to children's written and verbal abilities.

Reinforcing concepts

A recap of grammar and vocabulary concepts and terms ensures that old lessons are reinforced at every level and the child's recollection of concepts is refreshed before he or she embarks on new and more challenging exercises.

Speaking and listening exercises

These sections are designed to help students communicate in English with correct pronunciation. The exercises help the child to learn to speak with confidence and to listen carefully. The speaking sections give the child practice in diverse kinds of speaking, such as interviews, class discussions, describing, giving directions, and sharing information. The listening exercises teach a child to respond to various oral problems.

Writing exercises

Essential English has sections that will help students develop independent writing skills. Level-appropriate activities—such as writing stories, letters and paragraphs, book reviews, diary entries, invitation cards, thank-you notes—stimulate and encourage students to plan, expand and proofread their work.

Everyday English

This is a unique forum where students can apply the language to interact in day-to-day activities. Simple exercises, such as ordering food, giving directions and asking the time, help students to confidently speak in English, and learn the vocabulary and expressions appropriate for common life experiences.

Fun-filled activities

These learner-centred sections introduce children to entertaining and creative craft projects, crosswords, word games, logic and reasoning games, cracking codes and so on. Although presented as games, these exercises are a vital part of the learning process and help children learn essential language skills.

Encouragement to read more

Essential English 4 and *5* include a Read More section, which provides information about the author and the extract/story. It introduces children to more books by the same author or to other books in the same genre. This is to motivate children to find appropriate reading material that fits in with their interests from the school library.

Acquiring tools for independent learning

The children are taught to use the dictionary and thesaurus, to do basic research individually or in groups, and to present reports, all of which are independent learning skills crucial for middle and senior school.

With an understanding of the age-appropriate rules and elements that govern English, *Essential English* will help students to communicate correctly and effectively.

The Cemetery of the Chateau d'If 1

Edmond Dantes is wrongfully imprisoned for eighteen years in the Chateau d'If. This is the story of his daring escape.

On the bed lay a sack of canvas, and under its folds was stretched a long form—Faria, the cheerful companion with whom Dantes was accustomed to live so closely.

Alone—he was alone again—again condemned to silence!

"If I could die," he said, "I should go where he goes. Die? No, I want to live; I shall struggle to the very last; I will yet win back the happiness which has been taken away from me." Suddenly he arose, paced twice or thrice round the dungeon, and then paused abruptly by the bed.

"Just God!" he muttered. "Since none but the dead pass freely from this dungeon, let me take the place of the dead!" Without giving himself time to reconsider, he bent over the appalling shroud, opened it with the knife which Faria had made, and bore the corpse along the tunnel to his own chamber, laid it on his couch, once again kissed the ice-cold brow, turned the head towards the wall; entered the tunnel again, returned to the other cell, took from the hiding place the needle and thread, placing himself in the posture in which the dead body had been in the sack, and sewed up the sack from the inside.

---

condemned: punished
dungeon: dark prison or cell, usually underground
appalling: causing dismay or horror
shroud: a cloth or sheet in which a dead body is wrapped for burial
corpse: a dead human body

In the cemetery, he would allow himself to be covered with earth, and as it was night, the grave-diggers could scarcely have turned their backs before he would have worked his way through the yielding soil and escaped. If he was detected in this or the earth proved too heavy, he would be stifled, and then—all would be over.

At length, about the hour the governor had appointed, footsteps were heard on the stairs. Two men, approaching the bed, took the sack by its ends.

They deposited the supposed corpse on the bier. The party ascended the stairs. Suddenly he felt the fresh and sharp night air, and Dantes knew that the mistral was blowing. It was a sensation in which pleasure and pain were strangely mingled.

"Give us a light," said one of the bearers, "or I shall never find what I am looking for."

An exclamation of satisfaction indicated that the grave-digger had found the object of his search. Edmond heard a heavy metallic substance laid down beside him, and at the same moment a cord was fastened round his feet with painful violence.

The noise of the waves dashing against the rocks reached Dantes' ear distinctly as they went forward.

"Bad weather!" observed one of the bearers. "Not a pleasant night for a dip in the sea."

They ascended five or six more steps, and then they took him, one by the head and the other by the heels, and swung him to and fro. "One!" said the grave-diggers, "Two! Three!" And at the same instant Dantes felt himself flung into the air like a wounded bird, falling, falling, with a rapidity that made his blood curdle.

Dantes had been flung into the sea, and was dragged into its depths by a thirty-six-pound shot tied to his feet. The sea is the cemetery of the Chateau d'If.

---

cemetery: burial ground
yielding: productive, that which gives way
bier: a stand on which a coffin is laid before burial
mistral: a cold, northerly wind common in southern France
flung: thrown with force
made his blood curdle: horrified him

Reading Comprehension

Answer the following questions.

1. How did Dantes plan to escape?
2. What did Dantes feel and hear while inside the sack?
3. What went wrong with Dantes' plan?
4. What was the cemetery of the Chateau d'If?
5. What kind of story is this? Is it happy, funny, exciting or stressful?
6. What words has the author used to create the atmosphere?

Vocabulary

Classify the following nouns as masculine (M), feminine (F) or neuter (N).

heroine	☐	goose	☐	widow	☐
duke	☐	witch	☐	widower	☐
person	☐	monk	☐		

Choose words from the story which mean the opposite of the following.

shouted	________________	rewarded	________________
slowness	________________	yield	________________
appealing	________________	descended	________________

Grammar

Singular or plural nouns

> **Singular** means one of something. **Plural** means more than one.

Fill in the plural forms in the table below.

Singular	Plural
abacus	abaci
potato	
elf	
deer	
gallery	

Singular	Plural
hoof	
roof	
fish	
hippopotamus	
fly	

Concrete and abstract nouns

Concrete nouns refer to people, animals and objects.
Abstract nouns usually refer to feelings and ideas.

Underline the concrete nouns and circle abstract nouns in the following sentences.

My love is like a red, red rose.

The warmth of the fire made the room pleasant.

A clock tells you the time.

Shalini's best quality is her kindness.

Liberty and justice should be available to every citizen.

People should always tell the truth.

Summer in Delhi is uncomfortable because of the heat.

We were all impressed by the spaciousness of the house.

Spelling and Punctuation

Capital letters are used for:
- The first word in a sentence.
- Proper names.
- The first spoken word in a dialogue.

Full stops are used at the end of statements and commands.
Question marks are used at the end of questions.
Exclamation marks are used to end exclamations.
Commas are used:
- To signify a short pause.
- To separate words in a list.
- To separate spoken and unspoken words.

Rewrite the following sentences using correct punctuation.

1. where is anand's water bottle
2. everything looks beautiful
3. nandini ate the mushrooms
4. has iman come to school today
5. we won the match
6. it is bright and sunny outside
7. my mother and i are going to kartik's house
8. where have anoushka and savita gone

Writing

In this story, the central character is Edmund Dantes. The setting is the Chateau d'If. The plot is how Dantes escaped from prison.

Write a short story with central character: Uday Reddy; setting: Goa; plot: how he saved himself from a dangerous situation.

Listening

Your teacher will read out a few sentences. Which of them are true and which are false?

Speaking

Feeling the mistral gave Dantes a feeling of pleasure and pain together.
What gives you pleasure? What gives you pain? Discuss with your partner. Ask him/her the same questions.

Activity

Word game

In five minutes, how many words can you make with the letters in the box?
Every word must contain the letter E.

<table>
<tr><td colspan="2" rowspan="2">E</td><td>M</td><td>N</td></tr>
<tr><td>W</td><td>F</td></tr>
<tr><td>P</td><td>T</td><td>F</td><td>H</td></tr>
<tr><td>A</td><td>B</td><td>L</td><td>R</td></tr>
</table>

Read More

If you enjoyed this story, you could read the complete adventures of Edmund Dantes in *The Count of Monte Cristo* by Alexandre Dumas. Dumas also wrote other exciting adventure stories such as *The Three Musketeers* and *The Man in the Iron Mask*.

Yudhishtir the Just 2

The Mahabharata is one of the great Indian epics, about the rivalry and war between the Pandavas and Kauravas. Many years after the end of the war, the Pandavas decided to renounce the world. This is the story of that last journey told by Soma Guha.

The Pandavas were in the forest of Dvaita. Thirsty and out of breath, the five halted under a banyan tree. Nakul went to spot a source of water nearby. He soon arrived at a pool. As he was about to drink the water, Nakul was stopped by a voice.

"Not so fast, O son of Madri," it said. "You have to answer some questions first."

Nakul looked around but could see no one. Ignoring the voice, he drank some water. Very soon the prince fell down unconscious.

The same thing happened to Sahadev, when he went in search of Nakul.

Yudhishtir sent Arjun to investigate. Arjun arrived swiftly at the spot and was shocked by what he saw. What had happened to Nakul and Sahadev?

As Arjun dipped his hands in the pool, a voice spoke.

"Patience," it said. "Answer my questions before you taste the water of my pool."

Arjun turned back to the pool, drank some water and fell to the ground as well.

When Arjun failed to return, Yudhishtir sent Bheem to look for their missing brothers. Bheem reached the bank of the fateful pool. The sight of his unconscious brothers outraged him. He went towards the pool.

"Beware, Bheemsen, don't you dare touch the water," the voice resounded.

Seeing nobody around, Bheem started to drink the water. Immediately, he collapsed beside his brothers.

A few minutes later, Yudhishtir appeared on the scene. Beside the pool lay the bodies of the fallen princes. Yudhishtir went down on his knees and wept.

Yudhishtir was thirsty; he descended into the pool and cupped his palms.

"Wait, Yudhishtir," the voice said. "Your brothers fell as they did not pay heed to me. You are wiser. You will answer my questions before quenching your thirst in my pool."

"Ask me," he said quietly.

"Who is a happy person? What is the true path? What befriends the traveller?"

"Happy is the debtless person who lives in his own home and thrives on the simplest meal. The road that great men follow is the true path. Learning befriends the traveller."

"What is wisdom? What is patience? What is happiness?"

"Wisdom is to realise the true nature of every element. Patience is to stick to the righteous path. Happiness is the result of good conduct."

"What does one have to quit to ensure the love of all?"

"Pride."

"What does one have to lose to reap joy and not sorrow?"

"Anger."

"What does a man have to give up to become rich?"

"Desire."

"What is the greatest wonder in the world?" asked the Yaksha.

"Every day we see creatures die and yet we want to live forever. This is the greatest wonder in the world," said Yudhishtir.

"Thank you for answering me," the voice sounded pleased. "In return, I shall

---

outraged: angered
resounded: echoed loudly
quenching: satisfying
debtless: one who does not owe anybody anything
righteous: morally right

make one of your brothers come to life. Which one would you choose?"

After a moment of thought, Yudhishtir replied, "Nakul."

The Yaksha seemed hugely surprised. "Why Nakul?" he exclaimed. "Why not Bheem or Arjun?"

"Because it is right. A son of Kunti lives in me. A son of Madri should live as well. That is justice."

"Wonderful! Wonderful," the Yaksha declared.

Before the amazed eyes of Yudhishtir all his brothers slowly got to their feet.

Reading Comprehension

Answer the following questions.

1. Where were the Pandavas?
2. Why did Nakul, Sahadev, Arjun and Bheem fall unconscious?
3. What was the third question the Yaksha asked?
4. What answer did Yudhishtir give to the last question?
5. How did Yudhishtir surprise the Yaksha? What was the reason for his answer?
6. How did the Yaksha reward Yudhishtir for his sense of justice?
7. Do you think Yudhishtir made the right choice? Whom would you have chosen if you were in his position?

Vocabulary

Collective noun

A **collective noun** names a group of people, animals or things.

Match the following collective nouns to the people, animals or objects they describe. You can use a dictionary.

litter of	crows
flock of	academicians
brood of	sheep
faculty of	geese
board of	flowers
troupe of	kittens
choir of	acrobats
bouquet of	hens
murder of	singers
gaggle of	directors

Compound nouns

Compound nouns are nouns made up of two or more words. Usually the words are joined together. Sometimes they are connected with a hyphen or written as two separate words.

Rewrite the following sets of words as compound nouns.

mother + in + law = *mother-in-law*

bed + room = ______________________

under + ground = ______________________

full + moon = ______________________

tooth + paste = ______________________

head + master = ______________________

swimming + pool = ______________________

birth + day = ______________________

air + conditioner = ______________________

Grammar

Types of nouns

A **common noun** names any regular, ordinary person, animal, place or thing.

A **proper** noun names a very specific, very particular person, animal, place or thing.

A **concrete** noun refers to people, animals and objects.

An **abstract** noun usually refers to feelings and ideas.

Are the underlined nouns common or proper, collective, compound, concrete or abstract? The same noun can belong to more than one category.

The band of soldiers marched past, sweating because of the heat.

Anita enjoyed the softness of the kittens' fur.

The Indian Constitution promises freedom and equality.

Her father-in-law has a terrible illness.

During the safari we saw a pride of lions basking in the warmth of the sun.

Spelling and Punctuation

Syllables

Syllables are the building blocks of sounds that make up words.
For example, the word teacher is made up of two syllables: tea and cher.

Break up the following words into syllables.

It will be easier if you read the words aloud.

purple
control
jigsaw
triangle
classroom
coffee
cricketer
India
uniform
chocolate

How many syllables are there in the following words?

butterfly
principal
ambush
parantha
puppy
computer
banana
robot
jungle
syllable

Writing

The order in which things happen in a story is known as the sequence. The following sentences tell a story. But the sequence is wrong.

Number the sentences in the correct order to tell the story.

As soon as breakfast was over, I ran to my room to get ready. ☐

My mother had prepared a delicious breakfast. ☐

I had a bath and dressed in shorts and a t-shirt. ☐

We all drove to the lake together. ☐

On Sunday, I woke up late. ☐

I put a book and my camera into my backpack. ☐

Sitting by the lake we had a picnic. ☐

As we ate, my brother said we would all go to the lake today. ☐

Listening

Your teacher will read out a list of words. Point out the odd one in each list. Can you explain why the word is different?

Speaking

What is the one thing you cannot live without? Why?

Explain your reasons to the class. Also ask your classmates questions about the things they cannot live without.

Activity

Dictionary game

Use your dictionary to answer these questions. Give the meaning of each word.

1. What is the longest word beginning with ex?
2 What word directly follows lollipop?
3 What word comes directly before rhinoceros?
4 What is the very last word in the dictionary?
5 What is the fifth word in the im section?

Read More

There are many versions of the Mahabharata you could read. This extract is taken from Soma Guha's *Mahabharat: The War*. The first volume of Guha's retelling of the Mahabharat is called *The Game*.

3 *What's Eating You?*

Nature is not always wonderful! This story of vampire bats is by Nick Arnold.

"I can remember it like it was yesterday." The old man smiled, showing the gaps between his yellow teeth. The gaps made him hiss as he spoke. Like a snake.

"But when did it happen, grandpa?" asked the young boy with his eyes like saucers.

"It was in Brazil, back in 1927. We were there to study the wildlife and it was my first time in the jungle. I remember the strange sights and the smells but do you know what I remember most? The nights. The humming insects and the croaking frogs in the dark, smelly swamps. The wet chill in the air. The big round moon hiding amongst the trees."

"We made camp mostly around nightfall. Well, it gets dark quickly in the jungle and we had to light a fire and put our tents up in good time. Old Dr Beebe's orders. That's William Beebe of the New York Zoological Society, our expedition leader. And Dr B said we should always keep our feet inside the tents."

"Why did he say that, grandpa?"

"Well, because of the vampires, of course," hissed the old man.

"Vampires? Not real vampires like Count Dracula?" The boy's voice rose higher.

"Dracula wasn't no real vampire, Johnnie. He was a legend. But this is true. As true as I am sitting here. Real live vampire bats."

saucer: a small, shallow dish
vampire: a predator who drinks blood

The young boy gulped. "Bats! And do they really bite people?" he stammered.

"Sure they do and animals like cows and horses. Not dogs so much. Dogs can hear them coming. The bats flap down from the trees where they live silent as ghosts.

"They've got wings like old leather and huge ears to hear with. They creep along the ground to find your feet. Then they lick your toes to make sure they're nice and soft. And then they bite you!"

The boy looked over his shoulder nervously. "Do they really suck blood?"

"No, they lap it up like a cat laps milk. Or at least that's what Dr Beebe told us.

"Well, it was soon after that I got a rude awakening. I was in deep long sleep. Suddenly, I felt a sharp pain in my big toe like a needle. I shouted and then I was awake. Sweat streamed off me like a waterfall. It was dark but there was a moon and I saw a figure. Someone. Something."

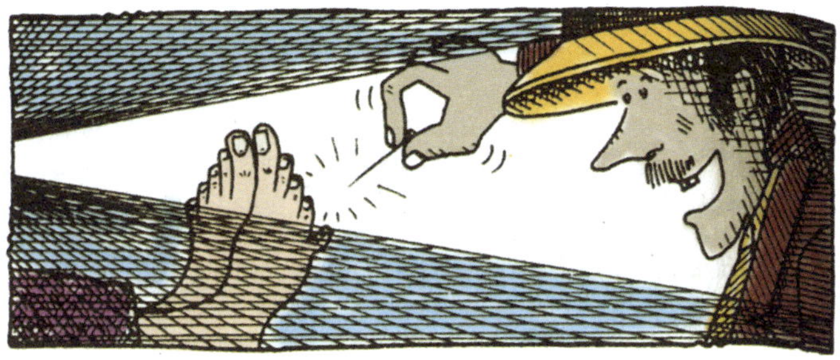

"Wasn't it a bat?"

"No—it looked human. I was scared, I don't mind telling you. I reached for the electric torch. Somehow I switched on the light and what do you think I saw? Dr Beebe. He was crouching there with a bright sharp pin in his hand. 'Sorry to disturb you, Jack,' he chuckles. 'Just trying a little test. I wanted to see if a vampire's bite would wake you.'

"Well, I was so shocked I just didn't know what to say.

"I got talking to some of the others the next day and it seems the doctor played the same trick on everyone. 'Practical research,' he called it.

"Well, the following night I slept really well. When I woke up I felt fine. Until I looked at my feet and saw the blood. Those pesky vampire bats had come by and I hadn't felt a thing!"

Grandpa drew off his scuffed brown shoe and then a worn green sock. His foot was white and blue veins criss-crossed the parchment-coloured skin. Years after the event his toes were still pitted with white scars. Bite marks.

pesky: troublesome
scuffed: roughened surface
pitted: marked or scarred

Reading Comprehension

Answer the following questions.

1. When did the incident narrated by the old man take place?
2. Why were the members of the expedition told to keep their feet inside the tents?
3. What do vampire bats eat?
4. Do the bats suck blood?
5. What woke grandpa in the night?
6. What was visible on grandpa's foot?

Vocabulary

Phobia comes from the Greek word for fear. Can you guess what the following phobia words mean?

Match the words to their meanings. You can use the dictionary.

arachnophobia	fear of women
gynophobia	fear of heights
hydrophobia	fear of loud noises
xenophobia	fear of enclosed spaces
autophobia	fear of being alone
acrophobia	fear of strangers
claustrophobia	fear of spiders
phonophobia	fear of water

Circle the odd word in each line.

bottle	jug	bucket	plate	glass
fire	water	wind	chair	earth
hot	cold	scared	warm	cool
book	handkerchief	magazine	newspaper	poster

Can you explain why the word you have circled is different from the others?

Grammar

Making sentences

A **sentence** is a group of words which starts with a capital letter and ends with a full stop **(.)**, question mark (?) or exclamation mark (!). A sentence contains a subject, an object and a verb.

Rearrange the following sets of words to make sentences. Keep in mind the punctuation.

1. Patel the Dehradun family to went a for holiday.
2. teapot my broken is mother's.
3. uncle too is your help to us busy.
4. papers desk the are on the.
5. outside the football are seniors playing.
6. seen my anywhere you have book new?
7. too is heavy me carry box for that to.
8. new look at bicycle my!

Types of sentences

There are four types of sentences:

An **assertive** sentence makes a statement.

An **imperative** sentence gives a command or makes a request.

An **exclamatory** sentence shows strong feelings.

An **interrogative** sentence asks a question.

Mark A against the assertive sentences, S against the imperative sentences, E against the exclamatory sentences and I against the interrogative sentences.

Did you enjoy the movie? ☐

Run inside before it starts to rain. ☐

It is a very cloudy day. ☐

The mountains are beautiful! ☐

You have grown taller! ☐

How many students forgot to bring their crayons? ☐

Please help the new student. ☐

Asha has fallen and hurt herself. ☐

Spelling and Punctuation

When we add a suffix beginning with a vowel to a word ending in a silent e, we remove the silent e.

Join the words below to their suffixes to create new words

hope + ing	=	*hoping*	globe + al	=	____________
love + able	=	____________	slave + ish	=	____________
square + ish	=	____________	achieve + able	=	____________
pile + ing	=	____________	love + ing	=	____________

When we add a suffix that begins with a consonant to a word ending in a silent e, we do not remove the silent e.

Join the words below with the suffixes given.

care + ful	=	____________	bare + ness	=	____________
love + ly	=	____________	confine + ment	=	____________
achieve + ment	=	____________	grace + ful	=	____________
hope + fully	=	____________	safe + ly	=	____________

Writing

This story tells us about a very unusual animal. Which is your favourite animal? Describe it in a short paragraph. Include details such as where it lives, what it eats and what it looks like.

Listening

Identify the animals based on the descriptions read out by your teacher.

Speaking

Vampire bats are found in South America. Would you like to visit South America? Write about your dream vacation.

Everyday English

After reading about the exciting wildlife camp in the story your class has decided to go for a weekend excursion.
Sit together as a group and plan out the details of the excursion.

You can discuss details like the following:

- Rohan, your job is to find out the camp details—the amenities, the costs involved, etc.
- Who will finalise the travel plans and the itinerary?
- Sharoma, will you make a list of what everyone should carry?

Activity

Shrinking words

Drop one letter at a time to make another word.

Each time you take away a letter, the remaining letters must spell a real word.

For example: gasps – gaps – gas – as – a

STARTLING ↓

STARTING ↓

________________ ↓

SATING ↓

________________ ↓

________________ ↓

SAT ↓

________________ ↓

Read More

If you enjoyed reading this story, you can find out more about nature's wonders in the book from which this is taken: *Horrible Science: Nasty Nature*. If you like reading about science, you can read the other books in the *Horrible Science* series.

Trees 4

This poem, by Joyce Kilmer (1886-1918), celebrates one of the most wonderful things ever created.

I think that I shall never see
A poem as lovely as a tree.

A tree whose hungry mouth is prest
Against the earth's sweet flowing breast;

A tree that looks at God all day,
And lifts her leafy arms to pray;

A tree that may in summer wear
A nest of robins in her hair;

Upon whose bosom snow has lain;
Who intimately lives with rain.

Poems are made by fools like me,
But only God can make a tree.

prest: poetic version of pressed
robin: a small bird with a red breast
intimately: closely

Reading Comprehension

Answer the following questions.

1. What do you think the "hungry mouth" of the tree is?
2. What does the poet mean by "leafy arms"?
3. How will the tree have "a nest of robins in her hair"?
4. Why do you think the poet refers to the tree as "her"?
5. Why does the poet call himself a fool?

Vocabulary

Find the antonyms of the following words in the grid below.

repel	________________	north	________________
absent	________________	hinder	________________
backward	________________	tight	________________
discourage	________________	wild	________________
safety	________________	smooth	________________

A	T	T	R	A	C	T	O	K	L
E	A	R	A	R	M	Q	U	I	B
N	M	H	E	L	P	H	M	Y	F
C	E	O	F	O	R	W	A	R	D
O	F	A	L	W	E	A	Z	O	A
U	E	R	A	C	S	X	E	U	N
R	A	S	I	N	E	B	E	G	G
A	L	L	Y	G	N	U	S	H	E
G	T	S	O	U	T	H	P	E	R
E	Y	L	T	L	O	O	S	E	S

Accept and except

Accept means to receive something, while except means that something is being excluded or left out.

Fill in the blanks with accept or except.

Please ________ this gift from us.

Everyone has come on time __________ John.

Pallavi could not _______ the job offer because the job was in another city.

We hope you will _______ this award.

We are not allowed to watch TV ________ on weekends.

___________ Kamini, all the children have seen the movie.

Grammar

Possessive noun

A **possessive noun** tells us who or what owns (possesses) something.

To make a singular noun possessive, add 's.

To make a plural noun possessive, check the last letter of the plural noun. If the last letter is s, just add an apostrophe ('). If the last letter is not s, add 's.

Fill in the blanks with the possessive form of the noun given.

Read carefully to identify whether the word in the brackets is singular or plural.

The _________ dog was big and friendly. *(*boss*)*

The __________ kite was stuck in a tree. *(*boys*)*

___________ parents are both teachers. (Kirti)

Have you seen __________ pencil box? (Cyrus)

The __________ uniforms were green and brown. (soldiers)

The ________ dresses were made out of my old frock. (dolls)

Ambika accidentally spilt coffee on ________ new shirt. (Rahim)

I try to remember my __________ birthdays. (friends)

Countable and uncountable nouns

There are two types of nouns:

Countable nouns are those you can count. They may be singular or plural.

Uncountable nouns are those you cannot count.

Classify the following nouns as countable or uncountable.

soil bottle air water fan heat door window fire zebra ambulance box rain foot

Countable	Uncountable

You cannot use a or a number before uncountable nouns, but you can use words and phrases such as some, any, much, a little, a lot of, a piece of and a cup of.

Identify the uncountable nouns in the following and make sentences with them.

music	chair	priest	beauty
furniture	milk	money	book

Spelling and Punctuation

Usually, when we add the suffixes -able or -ous to words ending in -ce or -ge, we keep the -e. For example: courage + ous = courageous

Join the following words to the suffixes given.

notice + able = ____________ change + able = ____________

advantage + ous = ____________ outrage + ous = ____________

knowledge + able = ____________ trace + able = ____________

love + able = ____________ service + able = ____________

Writing

Write a story beginning with the following lines:

"I had just taken my seat on the plane when suddenly ..."

Listening

Listen to the story that your teacher will read and answer the following question.

How is this possible?

Speaking

What do you like about the poem? Discuss with your partner.

You can use the words in the box.

rhyme rhythm image simile

Activity

Your favourite tree

Take a photograph or paint a picture of your favourite tree. Discuss with your class about some of the following.

- What kind of tree it is
- Whether it bears fruit or flowers
- How it changes every season
- Why it is your favourite tree

5 After Twenty Years

This short play is based on the story of the same name by O. Henry (real name William Sydney Porter, 1862-1910), a popular American writer.

A New York City policeman walks up an avenue. A man named Bob stands in the shadows of a dark doorway.

BOB : It's all right, officer. I'm just waiting for a friend.

POLICEMAN : Yes?

BOB : It's an appointment made twenty years ago. There used to be a restaurant here—Big Joe Brady's restaurant.

The man in the doorway strikes a match and lights his cigar. The light shows a pale, square-jawed face with keen eyes and a little white scar near his right eyebrow.

BOB : Twenty years ago, I dined here at Big Joe Brady's with Jimmy Wells, my best chum and the finest chap in the world. He and I were raised right here in New York. I was heading West to make my fortune. So, we made an appointment to meet each other twenty years from then, right here at Brady's restaurant.

POLICEMAN : It sounds pretty interesting. Seems like a long time between meets, though.

BOB : For a time we wrote letters. But then we lost track of each other. But Jimmy will meet me here if he's still alive. He was the truest, staunchest chap ever. I have come a thousand miles and it's worth it if my old partner turns up!

POLICEMAN : Did pretty well in the West, didn't you?

---

chum: a close friend
staunchest: firmest

BOB : You bet! I hope Jimmy has done half as well. He was kind of a plodder, though, good fellow that he was. I had to compete with some of the sharpest wits going to get my fortune.

POLICEMAN : I'll be on my way. Hope your friend comes around all right.

BOB : Good night, sir!

A fine, cold drizzle begins to fall. A tall man in a light overcoat crosses the street after a while.

MAN : Is that you, Bob?

BOB : Is that you, Jimmy?

MAN : It's Bob, sure as fate. I was certain I'd find you here if you were still alive. How has the West treated you, old man?

BOB : It has given me everything I asked for. You've changed lots, Jimmy. I never thought you were so tall. Are you doing well here, Jimmy?

MAN : Moderately. Come on, Bob, we'll go around to a place I know of, and have a good long talk.

NARRATOR : The two men walk up the street, arm in arm. Bob, flushed with success, tells his companion all about his career. Soon they pass a brightly-lit drugstore.

BOB : Hold on! You're not Jimmy Wells! Twenty years is not long enough to turn a man's eyes from brown to blue!

MAN : It can be long enough to turn a good man into a bad one. You are under arrest, "Silky" Bob. The Chicago police department thought you might be heading our way.

BOB (*sighs*) : I'll come quietly. But how did you know where to find me?

MAN : Here's a note I was asked to hand to you. It's from Patrolman Wells.

Bob reads the note.

POLICEMAN : Dear Bob, I was at the appointed place on time. When you struck the match to light your cigar, I recognised your face from a "wanted" poster sent from Chicago. Somehow I couldn't arrest you myself, so I went around and got a plainclothes detective to do the job.
Signed, Jimmy

---

plodder: one who works slowly and steadily
fate: something that unavoidably befalls a person, destiny

Reading Comprehension

Answer the following questions.

1. Who was Bob waiting for?
2. Why hadn't Bob seen Jimmy for twenty years?
3. How did Bob describe Jimmy to the policeman?
4. How did Bob find out that the man was not Jimmy?
5. What words would you use to describe Bob and Jimmy?

Vocabulary

Synonyms

Synonyms are words with the same or similar meanings.

List synonyms for the following words.

enough	________________	fate	________________
road	________________	interesting	________________
job	________________	fellow	________________

Affect and effect

Affect is usually a verb, meaning to change or to have influence on something. Effect is usually a noun. When you affect something, you have an effect on it.

Fill in the blanks with affect or effect.

Sonali wanted to become a journalist, and nothing could ________________ her decision.

The hot soup had an immediate __________ on my sore throat.

The dancer's success is the _________ of her hard work.

This movie will ________ you strongly.

The beautiful rainbow is the ________ of sunlight shining on water.

Your performance in this test will ________ your final results.

The older students are having a negative _______ on the juniors.

The weather had a terrible _______ on Khushi's cold.

Grammar

Phrases

A **phrase** is a group of words within a sentence that does not contain a subject and a predicate, and doesn't make sense by itself. For example, in the sentence, My father bought me a bicycle, a bicycle does not contain a subject and predicate.

Tick the phrases.

Of stone	☐	At the park	☐
In the morning	☐	Which was warm and comfortable	☐
We watched the sunset	☐	Of potatoes and onions	☐
With no time to spare	☐		

Rewrite the following sentences as questions.

1. Your new uniform is grey.
2. This will be our classroom next year.
3. I can have the red kite.
4. We will have a free period.
5. That is the new math teacher.
6. Your brothers are very tall.
7. We will have ice cream for dessert.
8. They will visit Algeria and Morocco.

Spelling and Punctuation

Use commas to punctuate the following sentences.

During our world cruise we visited Singapore Madagascar South Africa Brazil Mexico and Japan.

Ladies and gentlemen boys and girls welcome to the winter concert!

Vasundhara Chiragh and George will be performing a song.

Don't forget to buy flour eggs milk and sugar so that we can bake a cake.

On the farm there were pigs hens cows sheep and horses.

My brothers' names are Anirudh Harish Mihir and Karan.

Writing

Rewrite the first page of "What's Eating You" as a play.

Remember, in a play, one character cannot speak for a long time. Also, you have to show the listener's responses by adding exclamations or questions.

Listening

Your teacher will read out some words. Listen carefully and identify the silent letter in each word.

Speaking

Discuss your earliest memories with your classmates.

What is the earliest thing that you remember? How old were you at the time?

Everyday English

You are meeting an old friend for lunch.

Call up a restaurant and reserve a table for two persons.

You can use some of the sentences below:

- Is this the China House?
- My name is Gautam Sen.
- Can I book a table for two persons?
- For tomorrow, Thursday.
- At one o'clock.
- Please make the reservation in the name of Gautam Sen.
- Thanks.

Activity

Word change

Make one word into another by changing one letter at a time.

GIRL	DIET	WALLS
↓		
GILL	________	________
↓		
MILL	________	________
↓		
MILE	________	________
↓		
MALE	CARE	TIGER

Read More

If you enjoyed this play, you can read short stories by O. Henry.

6 I'm Only a Child

At the Earth Summit at Rio Centro in Brazil (1992), Severn Suzuki spoke on behalf of the Environmental Children's Organisation. She asked the adults there to change their ways, so that the world would be a better place for future generations.

Hello, I'm Severn Suzuki speaking for ECO, the Environmental Children's Organisation. We are a group of twelve- and thirteen-year-olds from Canada trying to make a difference: Vanessa Suttie, Morgan Geisler, Michelle Quigg and me.

We raised all the money ourselves to come six thousand miles to tell you adults you must change your ways. Coming here today, I have no hidden agenda. I am fighting for my future. Losing my future is not like losing an election or a few points on the stock market. I am here to speak for all generations to come.

I am here to speak on behalf of the starving children around the world whose cries go unheard. I am here to speak for the countless animals dying across this planet because they have nowhere left to go. We cannot afford to be not heard. I am afraid to go out in the sun now because of the holes in the ozone. I am afraid to breathe the air because I don't know what chemicals are in it.

I used to go fishing in Vancouver with my dad until just a few years ago we found the fish full of cancers. And now we hear about animals and plants going extinct every day—vanishing forever.

---

agenda: plan
ozone: layer of earth's protective atmosphere
extinct: dying or vanishing forever

In my life, I have dreamt of seeing the great herds of wild animals, jungles and rainforests full of birds and butterflies, but now I wonder if they will even exist for my children to see.

Did you have to worry about these little things when you were my age? All this is happening before our eyes and yet we act as if we have all the time we want and all the solutions.

I'm only a child and I don't have all the solutions, but I want you to realise, neither do you!

You don't know how to fix the holes in our ozone layer.

You don't know how to bring salmon back up a dead stream.

You don't know how to bring back an animal, now extinct.

And you can't bring back forests that once grew where there is now desert.

If you don't know how to fix it, please stop breaking it!

Here, you may be delegates of your governments, business people, organisers, reporters or politicians—but really you are mothers and fathers, brothers and sisters, aunts and uncles—and all of you are somebody's child.

I'm only a child, yet I know we are all part of a family, five billion strong, in fact, 30 million species strong and we all share the same air, water and soil—borders and governments will never change that. I'm only a child, yet I know we are all in this together and should act as one single world towards one single goal.

In my anger, I am not blind, and in my fear, I am not afraid to tell the world how I feel.

delegate: a person sent to represent a larger group

Reading Comprehension

Answer the following questions.

1. Who was Severn Suzuki? Which organisation did she represent?
2. Why did Severn feel she was losing her future?
3. What was Severn's reason for speaking at the summit?
4. "If you don't know how to fix it, please stop breaking it!" What is Severn referring to?
5. What is the main idea of Severn's speech? Do you agree with her?

Vocabulary

Change the following verbs from the past tense to the present tense.

I saw three fluffy white clouds. ______________________

Kamini was reading a mystery story. ______________________

My sister studied at a medical college. ______________________

The boys were playing football in the garden. ______________________

Shiv was doing his homework quietly. ______________________

Everyone went out for a walk. ______________________

Rahul did not play tennis. ______________________

We were a very big family. ______________________

Change the verbs from the present tense to the past tense.

We are going to the museum this morning. ______________________

Mallika and Arun have a new game to play with. ______________________

Varun and I are watching the football match. ______________________

The baby is sleeping in his crib. ______________________

The three kittens are playing in the garden. ____________________

The gardener does his work very well. ____________________

Amit is milking the cow. ____________________

My mother feeds the dog. ____________________

Grammar

Doing verbs and helping verbs

Doing verbs are verbs which show that the subject was doing a particular action. For example, Hari was playing. Here playing is what Hari was doing.

Helping verbs are verbs which are used along with another verb. Be, do and have are the common helping verbs. In Hari was playing, was is the helping verb.

Underline the doing verbs.

We heard a strange noise coming from under the bed.

Anu and Sandeep talked to each other on the phone for three hours.

I cheered for Nandini during her tennis match.

They are all going to Shimla for the weekend.

Amrita will win the election.

Underline the helping verbs.

I walk faster than you do.

Rohan has finished his work.

We will go home early today because it is Saturday.

Do you like boiled eggs?

You were working very hard yesterday.

Identify the tense of the following sentences. Rewrite the sentences based on the instructions given in the brackets.

1. They are very strong. *(Change to simple past tense)*
2. We will finish it on time. *(Change to simple present tense)*

3. This is our family home. *(Change to simple future tense)*
4. Your father will be busy. *(Change to simple past tense)*
5. Sanjana played by herself in the garden. *(Change to simple future tense)*

Spelling and Punctuation

Read aloud the following words.

scorch	scale	sketch	risk
scare	scone	skull	brisk
scorn	scratch	sky	ask
scar	disc	skin	tusk
scalpel	skim	skeleton	

Writing

Write a formal letter to your local Residents' Welfare Association suggesting some environment-friendly policies.

Listening

Your teacher will read out some questions. How many of them can you answer?

Speaking

Imagine you are making a speech at an international forum. What issue would you talk about?

Make a speech to your class. Your speech should be two minutes long.

Activity

Word origins

Use a dictionary that gives word origins to find out where these words came from and what they mean.

toucan	gazette	yacht	anthology
chocolate	spaghetti	dandelion	bandicoot

7 Don't Do As I Say

The tales of Mulla Nasruddin, a legendary wise man from somewhere in the Middle East, have been retold all over the world. This story is written by Shahrukh Hussain.

Mulla Nasruddin was famous for being a bit odd. You could say that his mind worked very differently from that of other people. He thus behaved in a way that people often found strange and hard to understand. Some put it down to the fact that he came from Sivrihisar. Everyone knew the people of that region were very strange. They dressed strangely and they talked strangely and their entire conduct was strange. But most wise men agreed that beneath the apparent foolishness of Mulla Nasruddin was clarity of insight that cut straight to the heart of the truth. Sometimes though, one had to ponder before one understood the inner wisdom of his remarks and ways.

When Nasruddin was a boy, he helped his father carry merchandise back and forth from the cities where the goods were made to those where they were sold. Even then, Nasruddin did exactly as he wanted and not as he was told to. If he did not agree with what he was commanded to do, he would do things his own way—even if it was his father's orders he was disobeying.

"What is wrong with the boy?" spluttered Nasruddin's father in exasperation to his wife and friends. "He does exactly the opposite of what I say."

clarity: clearness
insight: understanding
ponder: think carefully
merchandise: manufactured goods
exasperation: extreme annoyance

"Then the best thing is to reverse your commands," everyone advised. "Tell him you want him to go right if you wish him to go left and command him to stand still when you want him to walk on."

So that is what the old merchant did.

On the whole, this method worked reasonably well. Nasruddin galloped along at a great speed when his father asked him to slow down, and loaded the goods on to the donkeys when he was told to leave them in the store, and remained very quiet when his father invited him to converse. And so the partnership became very workable though the old man wished that he did not have to work in such a contrary way just to get the simplest things done smoothly.

One day, as Nasruddin and his father were driving their donkeys across a fast-moving stream, the pannier on the back of one of the donkeys began to slip.

"Nasruddin!" yelled the old merchant, thinking hard to frame his command so that it was the opposite of what he wanted done. "Quick! The bags of flour are slipping into the water. Press down on them!"

Immediately, Nasruddin reached out and pressed hard on the pannier carrying the flour. The fastening unloosened with his weight, and the bags of flour came away and fell into the river.

"Heavens, boy!" yelled Nasruddin's father. "Why, in the name of Almighty God, did you do that?"

Nasruddin looked into his father's face. "Because, Father, I thought you should realise how foolish your orders are."

contrary: opposite in nature; strange
pannier: a large basket for carrying goods

Reading Comprehension

Answer the following questions.

1. What was Mulla Nasruddin famous for?
2. What did wise men think of Nasruddin?
3. What advice did Nasruddin's father's friends give him? Why?
4. What did Nasruddin's father order Nasruddin to do when he saw the pannier slipping?
5. Why did Nasruddin carry out his father's order?
6. Is this story funny? Why do you think so?

Vocabulary

Adverbs

Adverbs are used to describe verbs. Some pairs of adverbs and verbs are often used together.

Match the following adverbs and verbs.

Adverb	Verb
totally	whispered
completely	ran
softly	forgot
hopefully	asked
quickly	agree

Verb contractions

Verb contractions are sets of words (containing a verb) that are shortened into a single word. For example: was + not = wasn't.

Use verb contractions to replace the underlined words. Remember to use apostrophes in the correct places.

Navin <u>was not</u> at home when I went to visit him. ____________

My sister <u>does not</u> like milk. ____________

They will be practicing for the concert this evening. ______________

I have been writing a short story. ______________

Saumya says she will bring the work tomorrow. ______________

Ashwin says he is very busy. ______________

You are the best bowler on the team. ______________

They said they would help us. ______________

The teacher said she had been ill. ______________

They will bring the new books to school tomorrow. ______________

I would love to help you. ______________

We have been dancing to a new song. ______________

Grammar

Tenses

Tenses can show the time of a verb's action or being. Time can be split into three periods—the present, the past and the future.

The tenses are simple, continuous and perfect.

The **simple tense** is used to show permanent characteristics of people and events or what happens regularly or in a single completed action.

The **continuous tense** is used when talking about a particular point in time.

The **perfect tense** gives a little bit more information about an action or state. It is used when an action or situation in the present is linked to a moment in the past. It is often used to show things that have happened up to now but are not finished yet or to emphasise that something happened but is not true anymore.

Identify the tenses in the following sentences.

The other students are teasing Asha. ______________

Yesterday I was polishing my shoes. ______________

Next year she'll be working in Egypt. ____________________

They were jumping on the trampoline. ____________________

I was climbing trees in the park. ____________________

We are going to bake cookies. ____________________

Soon you will be going to college. ____________________

Tara is learning how to swim. ____________________

Tomorrow we will be starting a new story. ____________________

The animals at the zoo were acting very strangely. ____________________

Positive and negative sentences

Positive sentences tell us what something (or someone) does, is, or has.
Negative sentences tell us what something is not, does not do, or does not have.

Rewrite the following negative sentences as positive ones.

I don't like to eat spinach *I like to eat spinach.*

The water isn't cold enough. ____________________

The kittens are not black. ____________________

Abhishek hasn't got an older sister. ____________________

You haven't turned the lights off. ____________________

They don't want to sell their house. ____________________

Rewrite the following positive sentences as negative ones.

Remember that you can use verb contractions in place of phrases such as is not, does not or has not.

1. Your school bag and cricket bat are on the table.
2. Prem and Kiran play tennis.
3. The dog is digging holes in the garden.
4. Their father has come to visit them.
5. I want to watch the cricket match.
6. Sahil has finished his homework.

Spelling and Punctuation

When we add a suffix to a word ending in y where the letter before y is a consonant, we usually remove the y and use i instead. For example:

lazy + ness = laziness

Join the following words and their suffixes to make new words.

dry + ed	=	______	multiply + ed	=	______
duty + ful	=	______	plenty + ful	=	______
beauty + fy	=	______	fry + es	=	______
army + es	=	______			

When we add a suffix to a word ending in y where the letter before y is a vowel, we usually do not remove the y or add an i. For example: annoy + ed = annoyed

Join the following words and their suffixes.

play + ful	=	______	coy + ness	=	______
buoy + ant	=	______	destroy + ed	=	______
bray + ed	=	______			

Writing

Write an informal letter to a friend inviting him/her to come and visit you during the summer holidays.

Listening

Listen to the story and answer the following question.

Where do you think the spectacles were?

Speaking

Do you know any riddles? Ask your partner a riddle and see if he/she can answer.

Can you answer your partner's riddles?

Activity

Mystery word

Can you work out the mystery word?

Clues

Grass around the house	3 ☐	2 ☐	6 ☐	9 ☐					
Part of the foot	1 ☐	7 ☐	7 ☐	4 ☐					
Where a mouse lives	1 ☐	5 ☐	3 ☐	8 ☐					
The world's largest mammal	6 ☐	1 ☐	2 ☐	3 ☐	8 ☐				
Mystery word	1 ☐	2 ☐	3 ☐	4 ☐	5 ☐	6 ☐	7 ☐	8 ☐	9 ☐

Read More

If you enjoyed this story, you can read the book from which it is taken: *The Wisdom of Mulla Nasruddin* by Shahrukh Hussain.

He Wishes For the Cloths of Heaven 8

This is one of the best-known poems by William Butler Yeats (1865-1939), the Nobel Prize-winning Irish poet and dramatist.

Had I the heavens' embroidered cloths,
Enwrought with golden and silver light,
The blue and the dim and the dark cloths
Of night and light and the half light,
I would spread the cloths under your feet:
But I, being poor, have only my dreams;
I have spread my dreams under your feet;
Tread softly because you tread on my dreams.

enwrought: worked with something by way of decoration
tread: step or walk on

Reading Comprehension

Answer the following questions.

1. Who is the "he" in the title?
2. What do you think are the "cloths of Heaven"?
3. Do you think the poet's dreams are really under someone's feet? What do you think the dreams are being compared to?
4. What do you notice about the sets of rhyming words in this poem?

Vocabulary

Participles

The **base form** of a verb is its most simple form such as bite, wake, sleep, jump and play.

Participles are verbs which are used as adjectives. For example, in the phrase the closed door, closed describes the state of the door.

The **past participle** form of a verb may end in -d, -ed, -n, -en or -t. For many verbs the past participle form is the same as the past tense form.

The table below shows the base, past tense, and past participle forms of verbs.

Fill in the missing words

Base Form	Past Tense	Past Participle
	knew	known
	filled	filled
fly		flown
fall	fell	
pay		paid
write	wrote	
bite	bit	
		eaten
	went	
begin		begun
drive	drove	

Grammar

Identify the tenses in which the following sentences are written.

We have been drawing a picture. ____________________

Rama had been going to the doctor. ____________________

I have had my bath. ____________________

He will have gone to bed by 10 o'clock. ____________________

They had gone to buy new shoes. ____________________

Tomorrow, we will have been friends for five years. ____________________

Spelling and Punctuation

When we add -ing to words ending in ie, we replace ie with -y.

Join the following words and their suffixes.

lie + ing = *lying*

tie + ing = ____________________

die + ing = ____________________

Speaking

Bring your favourite poem to class and read it out to your classmates.

9 All About Stars

How much do you know about galaxies and constellations? Find out in this series of questions and answers by acclaimed science writers Gilda and Melvin Berger.

Is each star alone in space?

No, every star belongs to a large group of stars called a galaxy. Each galaxy has between a billion and a trillion stars. And there are about 50 billion galaxies throughout the universe. Our sun is part of a galaxy called the Milky Way.

Astronomers say that the Milky Way galaxy contains 100 billion stars.

When you look up on a clear dark night, you can see part of the Milky Way. It is a band of hazy white light across the sky. To people long ago it looked like a splash of milk, so they named it the "Milky Way".

How big is the Milky Way galaxy?

Too big to be easily measured in miles or kilometres. Instead, astronomers measure the distance in light-years. A light-year is the distance that light, which moves at 186,000 miles (297,600 km) a second, travels in one year. A light-year is just less than 6 trillion miles (9.6 trillion km). The distance across the Milky Way galaxy is about 100,000 light-years—or 6 million billion mile (9.6 million billion km)!

Is the sun near the centre of our galaxy?

No, the sun is off to one side.

Our galaxy is shaped like a gigantic pinwheel with a bulge in the centre. The arms of the pinwheel extend out from the bulge. The sun is in the arms. It is about 33,000 light-years from the centre.

The sun and all the stars are moving around the centre of the galaxy. The sun travels at a speed of about 156 miles (250 km) a second. At that speed, it takes 250 million years for the sun to complete one giant loop around the Milky Way.

Can we see other galaxies besides the Milky Way?

We can see three other galaxies without a telescope. Each looks like a hazy patch of light in the night sky.

From the Northern Hemisphere we can see the Andromeda galaxy. It is 2,200,000 light-years away. Andromeda is even bigger than the Milky Way galaxy.

From the Southern Hemisphere we can see two galaxies called the Large and Small Magellanic Clouds. They are respectively 160,000 and 180,000 light-years from the earth.

How far is the most distant galaxy?

Scientists believe it is about 13 billion light-years away—a distance of 80,000,000,000,000,000,000,000 miles (128,000,000,000,000,000,000,000 km)! Some say this may be the edge of the universe. Others believe the universe may not even have a boundary.

Astronomers know that all the galaxies in the universe are rushing away from each other today. But no one knows that all the galaxies in the universe are rushing away from each other today. But no one knows if this will continue forever or if they will start coming together in time.

Is a constellation the same as a galaxy?

No. A constellation is a group of perhaps a dozen bright stars—and many more stars that are not as bright—all in the same area of the sky. A galaxy, you know, has billions of stars stretched over a much greater distance.

Long ago, people looked in wonder at the groups of stars that make up the constellations. In their minds they drew lines joining the stars—just like connect-the-dot puzzles—to make pictures in the sky. Some of the pictures were of legendary figures, such as Hercules and Pegasus. Others were of animals, such as Taurus the bull. Astronomers have divided the sky into eighty-eight constellations. They use them to locate objects in the night sky, just as you use addresses to locate houses. Constellations also help tell directions at night.

Reading Comprehension

Answer the following questions.

1. What is a light-year?
2. What is a galaxy?
3. What is a constellation?
4. Will all galaxies some day become one?
5. Why are galaxies called Hercules and Pegasus?

Vocabulary

Below are the names of some famous foods and the countries they come from. Match the food to the country by colouring the boxes in the same shade. Use different colours for different sets of words.

taco	hamburger	jerk chicken	Mexico
Italy	Yorkshire pudding	sushi	England
Japan	pasta	Jamaica	USA

Similes

Similes are phrases that compare two ideas, using the words like or as.

Fill in the blanks below to make similes of your own. Be creative!

as big as ______________

as loud as ______________

as clean as ______________

as soft as ________________

jump like a _____________

scream like a _______________

sing like a _____________

see like a ___________

Can you use the following similes in sentences?

1. eyes like a hawk
2. as hard as nails
3. as smooth as silk
4. swim like a fish
5. as bright as sunlight

Grammar

Parts of a sentence

The basic parts of a sentence are the **subject**, **object** and **verb**.

Identify the subject, verb and object in the following sentences and write it in the correct column in the table below.

Samir threw the ball to Vishal.

I put the clothes into the cupboard.

The rabbit hopped through the garden.

The students begged for a free period.

Annie beat Shruti in the obstacle race.

Arnab twisted his ankle.

Malini cut off all her hair.

The thief stole the lady's handbag.

Subject	Verb	Object

Transitive and intransitive verbs

Transitive verbs are verbs that need a direct object for their meaning to be complete.

For example, in He broke the lamp, the verb broke requires an object (the lamp) in order for it to have a meaning.

In the sentence The boy ran, ran does not require an object. This is an example of an **intransitive verb**. Transitive verbs are followed by an object, while intransitive verbs are not.

Classify the verbs as transitive or intransitive.

The examinee answered correctly. ____________________

Every morning the sun rises. ____________________

The children play with a ball. ____________________

Flavia always cries. ____________________

Amir lost his homework. ____________________

The soldiers marched quickly. ____________________

We all smelled the beautiful roses. ____________________

My ankle hurts. ____________________

Spelling and Punctuation

Apostrophes

An apostrophe (') usually represents the missing letters when you contract words. Apostrophes are also used in possessive nouns, to show ownership.

Insert apostrophes in the correct places.

Sharmila wasnt feeling well on Wednesday so she couldnt go to the party.

Aditi didnt want to miss the party.

We all travelled in Vineets car.

Vineet said hed planned to invite the whole class.

I promised Id help to make the food.

We hadnt been to a party in a long time.

We cut a cake because it was Anees birthday.

We were sad that Sharmila wasnt there.

Rewrite the following sentences using apostrophes.

Kritika is reading the book that belongs to Alok.

Rajiv does not like to play with us.

Yasmin could not see the pet rabbit belonging to Mansi.

My grandmother would not let us play until we had cleaned the bedroom.

I cannot do this sum.

Arunima will not come to class this week.

You should not take things belonging to other people.

We will all go to meet the elder brother of Renuka.

Writing

Write a summary of “All About Stars” in about 100 words.

Remember to leave out unnecessary details and examples.

Listening

Your teacher will read the names of some professions. Listen carefully, and as each name is called out pretend to do the job.

Speaking

What do you think is the most important discovery in the world?
Discuss this topic with your classmates. Give reasons for your answers.

Everyday English

You want to visit the stars and the planets. You have a ticket and are at the airport check-in counter.

Practice a dialogue with the airline clerk. You can take turns with your partner.

CLERK: Good morning. May I know your flight details?

YOU: ...

CLERK: Yes, that's right. I need your passport and your ticket, please.

YOU: ...

CLERK: Thank you. Do you have any luggage to check in Mohan?

YOU: ...

CLERK: Can you put them on the conveyor belt, please?

YOU: ...

CLERK: Would you like a window or an aisle seat?

YOU: ...

CLERK: Here are your luggage tags and your boarding card. Your seat is 36B.

YOU: ...

Activity

Man words

Man is everywhere in this collection of words. Can you figure out the words?

MAN __________________ : person in change of large shop

MAN __________________ : juicy fruit

MAN __________________ : nail treatment

MAN __________________ : capital of Philippines

MAN __________________ : large house

MAN __________________ : instruction book

Read More

If you enjoyed this article, you can read the book from which it is taken: *Do Stars Have Points?* by Melvin and Gilda Berger.

Melvin and Gilda Berger have also written many other science books for children.

In the Fog 10

The famous detective, Sherlock Homes, investigates the alleged curse on the house of the Baskervilles.

The night was clear and the stars shone cold and bright. Before us lay the dark bulk of the house, its serrated roof and bristling chimneys. The servants had left the kitchen. There only remained the lamp in the dining room where the two men, the murderous host and the unconscious guest, still chatted over their cigars.

Every minute the white woolly plain, which covered one half of the moor, was drifting closer to the house. The far wall of the orchard was already invisible, and the trees were standing out of a swirl of white vapour. Holmes stamped his feet in impatience.

"If he isn't out in a quarter of an hour the path will be covered. In half an hour we won't be able to see our hands in front of us." They moved back upon higher ground, half a mile from the house.

Holmes dropped on his knees and clapped his ear to the ground. "Thank god, I think that I hear him coming."

serrated: having a jagged edge
bristling: visibly roused or stirred
moor: open wasteland

A sound of quick steps broke the silence of the moor. The steps grew louder, and through the fog, as through a curtain, there stepped the man whom we were awaiting.

As he walked he glanced continually over either shoulder, like a man who is ill at ease.

"Look out! It's coming!" cried Holmes.

The cloud was within fifty yards of where we lay, and we glared at it, all three, uncertain what horror was about to break from the heart of it. I glanced for an instant at Holmes' face. It was pale and exultant, his eyes shining brightly in the moonlight. But suddenly they started forward in a rigid, fixed stare, and his lips parted in amazement. I sprang to my feet, holding my pistol, my mind paralysed by the dreadful shape which had sprung out upon us from the shadows of the fog. A hound it was, an enormous coal-black hound.

With long bounds the huge black creature was leaping down the track, following hard upon the footsteps of our friend. Then Holmes and I both fired together, and the creature gave a hideous howl, which showed that one at least had hit him. He did not pause, however, but bounded onward. Far away on the path we saw Sir Henry looking back, his hands raised in horror, glaring helplessly at the frightful thing which was hunting him down.

Never have I seen a man run as Holmes ran that night. We heard scream after scream from Sir Henry and the deep roar of the hound. But the next instant Holmes had emptied five barrels of his revolver into the creature's flank. With a last howl of agony and a vicious snap in the air, it rolled upon its back, four feet pawing furiously, and then fell limp upon its side. The giant hound was dead.

Sir Henry lay where he had fallen.

"My god!" he whispered. "What was it?"

"It's dead, whatever it is," said Holmes. "We've laid the family ghost once and forever."

It was not a pure bloodhound and it was not a pure mastiff; but it appeared to be a combination of the two—gaunt, savage, and as large as a small lioness.

exultant: joyful and proud
hound: large dog
hideous: frightful
flank: the side of an animal between the ribs and hip
vicious: spiteful; malicious
pawing: moving the paws
mastiff: large, powerful
gaunt: extremely thin and bony

Reading Comprehension

Answer the following questions.

1. Who were in the dining room of the house?
2. What was the "white woolly plain"?
3. Why was Holmes impatient?
4. What horrific sight did Holmes and Watson see?
5. How was Sir Henry saved from the creature?
6. How does the author create an atmosphere of mystery and suspense?

Vocabulary

Homophones

Homophones are words which sound the same but have different meanings.

Select the correct word from the brackets to complete the following sentences.

Every year the farmer must _____________ the sheep. (sheer/shear)

The poor donkey had to carry a heavy ________ on his back (load/lode)

They were lost for hours as they couldn't find a way out of the ___________________. (maize/maze)

We had a chocolate __________ for dessert. (moose/mousse)

The Sahara is a ___________ in the North of Africa (desert/dessert)

They tied up the parcel with strong ________. (chord/cord)

This summer my mother will show me how to __________ a scarf. (knit/nit)

The yellow part of an egg is called the ______. (yoke/yolk)

Homographs

Homographs are words which are spelt the same but have different meanings.

Underline the homographs and write the meanings.

Please put the objects on the shelf into this box. ____________________

I object to your mistreatment of the prisoners. ____________________

When you are introduced, bow politely. ____________________

I tied a pink bow in her hair. ____________________

Camels live in the desert. ____________________

How could he desert his own family? ____________________

Grandfather was bitten by a vampire bat. ____________________

He was hit over the head by a baseball bat. ____________________

Even a minute speck of dust in an oyster can turn into a pearl. ________________

Wait a minute, I'll be right with you. ________________

She wound the thread around her finger. ____________________

The doctor cleaned and bandaged the wound. ____________________

Grammar

Subject and predicate

A **sentence** is a group of words that expresses a thought. A sentence has a **subject** (noun, pronoun) and a **predicate** (verb).

Underline the subject and circle the predicate in the following sentences.

The walls were covered with posters and pictures.

Mrs Sethia is a very good cook.

The dog growled frighteningly at the postman.
This chair is very uncomfortable.
Amrita goes for a walk in the park every evening.
My new jeans are very tight.
You must read this book.
The puppy has chewed all the furniture legs.

Phrases

A **phrase** is a group of words that acts as a single unit within a sentence. For example, in the sentence the girl in the blue t-shirt is winning the race, the girl in the blue t-shirt is a single unit. In the tree at the other side of the park, the other side of the park is a phrase.

Underline the phrases in the following sentences.

The black kitten is in the garden.
The house is full of guests.
We will play hide-and-seek in the park.
The house around the corner has a green door.
Kanika was told not to jump up and down.
The beehive was covered in bees.

Spelling and Punctuation

Read the following words. Note which words end in -ible and which end in -able.

edible	sensible	affordable	valuable
convertible	terrible	washable	desirable
visible	compatible	understandable	fashionable
responsible	feasible	suitable	acceptable
possible	horrible	comfortable	debatable

Writing

Make a poster for the upcoming dance festival in your school.

Use colours to make your poster bright and attractive. Some of the information you could include might be: date, time, place, theme.

Listening

Listen to the story that your teacher will read and answer the following question.

How is this possible?

Speaking

Discuss your favourite book with your partner. What do you like about it?

Activity

Crossword

Can you identify these famous detectives from books and films and their creators?

ACROSS

2 An absent-minded inspector with special powers

4 A dog detective

5 Young American detective living in River Heights

6 Famous Bengali detective fiction writer

DOWN

1 Leader of the Five Find-outers

3 Agatha Christie's detective with the egg-shaped head

Read More

If you enjoyed this extract, you can read the book from which it is taken: *The Hound of the Baskervilles* by Arthur Conan Doyle. There are also many short stories about the various adventures of Sherlock Holmes.

11 The Boy Who Could Not Finish A

Nury Vittachi is a Sri Lankan poet and author.

The problem with me is that I cannot finish a.

This causes me great problems as you can.

So I have decided to.

You will never find.

I'm going to look for a job where I can communicate *without. I may become a sculptor like my mum was before she.*

So I am really just writing this note to say.

This is so.

Well, you know what I.

"I do," Rose Himani said loudly. "I know exactly what you mean." There was something about Jack's stop-start attempts in his letter to her that made her want to celebrate simple pleasures: such as speaking complete sentences.

Rose quickly dialled Ravi Bin's number. The two of them had put a radio frequency chip on Jack so that they could locate him when he ran away.

Rose and Ravi sat in Abe's Tea House, trying not to focus on the small boy staring at them from the noodle shop on the other side of the road.

The two teachers talked about the most difficult children they had to deal with.

"Angela," Ravi said suddenly, focussing over Rose's shoulder.

communicate: to speak

"Oh yes, Angela Vora: she never stops interrupting ..."

Ravi said quickly, "Hi, Angela, how are you?"

Rose turned her head and was surprised to see Angela. "Angela, what are you—"

"Doing here? This café belongs to my uncle."

Rose peered through the café window. Her eyes darted around as she looked for Jack Pavan.

"What's wrong?" Angela asked.

"Oh, nothing," Rose said. "We're trying to keep an eye on a young man who tends to go wandering. He was over there, at—"

"At the noodle shop?" Angela smiled. "I know him: Jack Pavan. And I know where he goes, too. He comes down here quite often, and always ends up in the Chai Bay graveyard."

Rose's mouth dropped open. "That's where—"

"His mother is buried," Angela interrupted.

The two teachers made their way to the cemetery.

They found Jack Pavan at his mother's grave. He was holding what looked like a toothpaste tube.

"What are you doing?" Rose asked. "Is that toothpaste?"

"It's a type of glue used by. Stone masons use this stuff for repairing. My mum made this statue of an. But you see, it's—"

"Damaged," said a girl's voice.

They turned to find Angela Vora there. "It's damaged. The tip of the tongue has snapped off."

Rose examined the angel's head closely. The angel on the grave was singing, but the tip of her tongue had been chipped off.

Jack held up a sliver of grey stone. "I've got the missing. It was right here, at my feet, the last time I. So I got this stuff and I'm—"

---

peered: to look searchingly
darted: moved suddenly
sliver: a small often sharp piece of wood or glass

"Going to glue it back on?" Angela asked.

Jack nodded.

So they all waited quietly. When Jack was done, the angel looked much better.

Rose imagined it had more of a smile, but decided that it must be her imagination playing tricks.

"I think it's going to be fine, now," Jack said. "Mum will be much happier."

The four of them stood looking at the statue for a few seconds.

"Let's celebrate," said Rose, taking out her purse.

"Yeah," Angela said. "Let's get—"

"Some ice cream," Jack interrupted.

Reading Comprehension

Answer the following questions.

1. What couldn't Jack do?
2. Why did Rose dial Ravi's number?
3. What was Rose and Ravi's profession?
4. What was wrong with Angela Vora?
5. Where was Jack? What was he doing?
6. Do you think Jack and Angela should become friends? Why?
7. Why do you think the story's title is incomplete?
8. Do you think the story has a happy ending? Why?

Vocabulary

Make similes using the form as ______ as ______ for the following adjectives.

as slow as ________________ as green as ________________

as thick as ________________ as fresh as ________________

as cold as ________________ as comfortable as ________________

as white as ________________ as pretty as ________________

Match the following pairs of words.

salt and	butter
pros and	gentlemen
give and	socks
now and	soul
ladies and	cons
tables and	then
shoes and	pepper
bread and	chairs
heart and	take

Grammar

Comparative adjectives

Comparative adjectives show the difference between two nouns by stating that one noun has more of a particular quality than the second noun.

Fill in the blanks with comparative adjectives using the words given.

The eucalyptus tree is ______________ than the other trees in the park. (tall)

Pears are ________________ than apples. (juicy)

Rishi is a ________________ debator than Ananya. (good)

Shreya's voice is _______________ than Pranay's. (loud)

Chennai is ______________ than Chandigarh. (warm)

Your pillows are ______________ than mine. (soft)

Diamond is __________________ than glass. (hard)

My brother's bedroom is ______________ than mine. (tidy)

Number adjectives

> **Number adjectives** give quantity to the noun. They answer the question How many ...?

In the following sentences, underline the number adjectives.

Nowadays few people can afford to buy big houses.

Some batsmen are left-handed.

Add a little salt to the flour when you make the dough.

A few of us are collecting money to donate to a charity.

If you eat so much chocolate you won't be hungry for dinner.

Many people left the movie hall during the interval.

Do you have any spare safety pins?

I want to invite all of the other students in the class to a party.

Spelling and Punctuation

Question tags

> **Question tags** are added to a sentence to ask the listener to confirm the statement.

Add the correct question tags to the following sentences.

Terence is a very good dancer, ____________?

Harpreet and Deepak are best friends, ______________?

You don't like chocolate, _______________?

We can play volleyball during the games period, ________________?

Nalini has travelled to Japan, ______________?

Minal is Hitesh's older sister, ______________?

Kasturi takes Bharatnatyam lessons, ______________?

Your little brother cannot read, _____________?

That school won the trophy last year, ______________?

You will keep the door locked, _________________?

Homophones

Note the spellings of the following sets of homophones.

grown/groan	loan/lone	dear/deer
hire/higher	flea/flee	whole/hole
tow/toe	bare/bear	

Writing

Which is your favourite restaurant? Write a paragraph reviewing the restaurant. Include the name of the restaurant, its location, the kind of cuisine and describe some of the dishes you like to eat there.

Listening

Your teacher will read some pairs of sentences. Identify the homophones in each pair and write them down.

Pay attention to the spellings of the homophones.

Speaking

What is your favourite food? What country or region does it come from?

Discuss your favourite foods with your classmates.

Everyday English

Pretend that you are visiting a shoe shop to buy a pair of shoes. Practice with your partner how to talk to the shopkeeper.

You can use the following sentences:

- Can I get a pair of black shoes?
- My size is 5.
- Oh no, not this one. I want something with laces.
- Is this pair available in black leather?

Activity

Proverbs

Change one letter in each word to find well-known proverbs.

Bitter lake that newer

____

She earls bind hatches thy work.

____

Love end wet like.

____

Then at pains is poems

____

Read More

If you enjoyed this story, you can read other books by Nury Vittachi, such as *Twilight in the Land of Nowhen* and *The World's Funniest Book of Poems*.

Three Characters 12

Anushka Ravishankar is an award-winning poet who is known for her funny poems.

Gregariyus is a friendly type
Unless you get too close–
For he sometimes tends to take a swipe
At the nearest human nose.

It's not that he's ungentle
Or a violent kind of creature,
He merely feels that the human nose
Is a most annoying feature.

Jokular is a winsome bloke
He dearly loves to tell a joke
Long shaggy-dog tales and quick, short ones
Limericks, elephant jokes and puns
His jokes would really be quite nice
If he didn't always repeat them twice.

Pusillanimuss is a timid sort
He's scared of things that grunt and snort
His only friend in the whole world is
The female–Poosillanimiss.

swipe: sweeping blow
bloke: man; fellow
grunt: to make a deep sound
snort: to make a loud sound from the nose

Reading Comprehension

Answer the following questions.

1. What do the words "gregarious", "jocular" and "pusillanimous" mean? Look them up in the dictionary.
2. What is the poem about?
3. What do you notice about the rhymes and verses?
4. What do you think the poet is doing in the poem?

Vocabulary

Prefixes

> **Prefixes** are added to the beginning of a word to make a new word.

Choose prefixes from the box and add them to the words below.

auto sub under it down il im

down + stairs = *downstairs*

_____ + pilot	= __________	_____ + mobile	= __________
_____ + legible	= __________	_____ + standard	= __________
_____ + stand	= __________	_____ + biography	= __________
_____ + fall	= __________	_____ + marine	= __________
_____ + way	= __________	_____ + grade	= __________
_____ + legal	= __________	_____ + literate	= __________
_____ + ground	= __________	_____ + matic	= __________

Grammar

Interrogative pronouns and adjectives

Interrogative pronouns are pronouns used to ask a question. They include what, which, who and whose. For example, in the sentence Who said that? the pronoun is who.

Interrogative adjectives are very similar to interrogative pronouns, but they are used along with a noun. For example, in the sentence Which books did you buy? which is an interrogative adjective, because it is used along with the noun books.

In the following sentences, identify whether the underlined word is an interrogative pronoun or an interrogative adjective.

What did you say? ______________________

Who has done this? ______________________

What role will you play? ______________________

Which ingredients need to be added? ______________________

Whose book is this ? ______________________

Who is at the door? ______________________

What time is the movie? ______________________

Which students came late to class? ______________________

Prepositions

Prepositions are words we use to show the relationship of a noun or a pronoun to another word in the sentence. They can be called place words because they often tell us the position of things.

Tick the correct preposition from the brackets.

My aunt has a small cottage (by/in) the river.

If you go (along/down) these stairs and (along/around) the corridor, you will come to the office.

The lost book was found (in/under) the table (by/under) the door.

Don't walk (under/through) the forest alone.

Everyone ran (towards/over) the fence to look (next to/at) the horse.

Can you jump (into/over) this chair?

Kiran sat (between/among) Kamini and Kirti.

The man (on/at) the bus came (by/from) France.

Spelling and Punctuation

Fill in the blanks with -tion or -sion to make words.

vi______	ten______	admis________
mo_______	subtrac______	prepara_______
preposi____	mis_________	fic______
punctua______	men_______	inva_____
man______	na________	crea______
pas_____	expan______	deci________
ac_______	explora______	

Writing

Create your own character, like the ones in the poem, and write four lines about it.

Bani Chatterjee and the Burden of Expectation 13

Bani Chatterjee is a special student going to a special school for the first time in this story by Samit Basu.

As the car drove in through the gates of the Calcutta School of Witchcraft and Wizardry, ISC affiliated, established 2009, my first exclamation was a disappointed "What?"

A clean, nondescript building in the suburbs.

I got out of the car, dragging my feet. My trunks walked out of the boot, bobbing up and down, full of eagerness and joy. What I'd give for normal, non-living, non-bouncy luggage …

My phone rang. I took the call.

"GET DOWN!!" screamed a woman's voice.

I dived to the ground.

The school building exploded. Noiselessly, spectacularly. Leaving me lying under a huge cloud of grey dust.

"What is your name, little girl?" asked a voice.

"Who wants to know?" I turned around.

It was a thin, sinister, pointy-bearded middle-aged man in a strange leopard-print body-suit.

"From your worst nightmares, it is I," he said in a deep, growly voice. "Jaguar Tong. But I mean you no harm, Bani—yet."

"You know my name?"

"A-ha! Show me your scar!"

"You're crazy."

"I have known of the Prophecy for thousands of

affiliated: associated
nondescript: of no definite type or kind
sinister: suggestive of evil or harm
growly: speaking in an angry or surly manner

years," said Jaguar Tong, gesturing dramatically. "I won't repeat the exact words, because they were in ancient Sumerian, but to sum up, there would come in a city under shadow, a girl named B'Anachah Taji, actually, but approximations are allowed—who would save the magical world from Ultimate Evil. She would have a scar in the shape of a circle on her forehead—well, I could always make you one. But—look, could you turn off your phone? That ringtone is driving me insane."

I took the call.

"SAY CHEESE!!" screamed a woman's voice.

"Cheese!" I said obediently.

"Noooo!" screamed Jaguar Tong as a large wedge of cheese appeared and fell on his head.

"That the best you've got?" he roared incredulously.

"That the best you've got?" I asked the mysterious phone lady.

"I know a spell that kills people," Tong said sullenly.

"That's nice," I said. "I know double-entry bookkeeping."

He looked terrified. Hah.

"EXTINCTO!" said the woman on the phone.

"Extincto?"

Jaguar Tong clasped his throat, coughed and disappeared in a puff of smoke.

A cloud of dust rose and swirled around me. I crouched, till the whistling and howling subsided. And then, I saw the school again.

Lots of children came running out—just your everyday average Calcutta school running amok, and if you haven't seen that, let me tell you it isn't pretty.

They hoisted me on their shoulders—and shouted lots of silly things, such as "Saviour!", "Selected One!", "All-India Topper!" and, for some reason, "Reinstate Ganguly!"

They carried me into their silly auditorium to this old, bearded guy. The chief wizard headmaster dude, I assumed. He wore ordinary clothes, not some kind of wizard nightie.

"Step forward, Bani Chatterjee," he wheezed. "All these years of waiting, and on your first day at school, could you have made a more dramatic entrance? For

---

approximations: rough estimations
incredulously: showing disbelief
bookkeeping: skill of keeping account books
clasped: clutched
amok: to rush about wildly
saviour: a person who saves
reinstate: to put back

you are the Selected One the Prophecy spoke of, and you will stand up in the face of Ultimate Evil. Are you ready to stand up and face your destiny, Bani Chatterjee?"

"Sorry?" I enquired. "Could you please repeat the question?"

He did.

"Um, no," I said. "I'm no saviour. I wanted to study accounts."

Reading Comprehension

Answer the following questions.

1. Who is the narrator of this story?
2. How did she escape the explosion?
3. Why did Jaguar Tong want to make a scar on Bani's forehead?
4. What made Jaguar Tong disappear?
5. Did Bani want to be a saviour?
6. Does this story remind you of others you have read?
7. What do you like about this story?

Vocabulary

Idioms

Do you know the meanings of the following idioms?

a dime a dozen
Greek to me
a slap on the wrist
back seat driver
cock and bull
give someone the slip
level playing field
the last straw

Match the following words to their meanings.

associated	very old
ominous	threatening or disturbing
antique	having no special characteristics
unexceptional	extremely important
gloomy	depressing
crucial	linked to

Grammar

Possessive pronouns and adjectives

Possessive pronouns are pronouns which show ownership of something. Mine, yours, hers, its, ours, theirs are all possessive pronouns.

Possessive adjectives are words which modify a noun by showing that it belongs to somebody or something. In the phrases my book, your car and our house, my, your and our are possessive adjectives. Note that possessive adjectives always occur with a noun.

Mark the underlined words as possessive adjectives or possessive pronouns.

What colour is your new bicycle? ____________________

The house at the end of the street is theirs. ____________________

Her dog is bigger than mine. ______________________

Is that his mother? ______________________

The yellow frock is hers. ______________________

Please don't take my things without asking. ______________________

Tell Ravi that the blue raincoat is his. ______________________

Their cricket team is not as good as ours. ______________________

Conjunctions

Conjunctions are connecting words.

Choose conjunctions from the box to complete the following sentences.

and but or because so that if although

Renuka can play tennis *and* badminton.

Hari cannot go on the trip ______________________ he has no money.

We want to play cricket ______________________ cannot.

I like to sleep late ______________________ she likes to sleep early.

He is taking his medicine ______________________ he will get better soon.

I am good friends with Rashi ______________________ with Sunaina.

I enjoy maths ______________________ I am not good at it.

My mother will cook my favourite meal ____________ I behave well at the party.

I don't like chocolate ____________ cake.

Spelling and Punctuation

Quotation marks

We use quotation marks when we are directly quoting what somebody said.

Punctuate the following sentences using quotation marks.

Where is your father? demanded the principal.

Have you seen my kitten? asked Anu, I can't find her anywhere.

The party is tomorrow, said Komal, and everyone is invited.

Hooray! No more lessons today! shouted the students.

I have twisted my ankle and now I can't walk, sobbed Tarun.

Go back to your seats and sit quietly, shouted the teacher.

Why have you made this mess? asked my mother.

Everyone shouted Hurrah! Three cheers for Tanya!

Writing

A blog is an internet-based diary, where you can write about your life, your thoughts and your activities for people across the world to read.

Write your imaginary blog.

Listening

Your teacher will read some sentences. Listen and identify the idiom in each sentence. Discuss what it means.

Speaking

Hold a debate in class with each student speaking for or against television.

Do you think that television is a good thing? Why or why not?

Activity

Group of three

Change one letter in each word to find words that belong together.

fish	:	tuba	puppy	herding
planets	:	garth	cars	menus
instruments	:	tuna	wipes	mass

14 Alexander Graham Bell

The story of what lies behind an invention is often surprising, as in this story of the invention of the telephone, as told by Dr Michael Goldsmith.

Alexander Graham Bell invented the telephone, and it made him very rich and very famous.

Aleck, as he was called, was born in 1847. His mother was deaf so Aleck was keen on helping deaf people. His father was a teacher of the deaf, and was also very interested in the science of speech.

Aleck stayed with his granddad in London for a year. Grandad Bell was a speech scientist like Aleck's father, and he introduced fifteen-year-old Aleck to science.

Aleck met a scientist called Charles Wheatstone. Charles showed Aleck a machine that spoke! Actually, it wasn't that scary: more of a box of tricks really, which Wheatstone had built partly to demonstrate how different speech sounds are made, but mostly just for fun.

Back in Edinburgh, Aleck's dad challenged him to build a speaking machine. Aleck loved the idea, but in the end he made do with rubber lips and cheeks and teeth made of a plastic-like material, cast from a human skull.

In 1863, Aleck started his teaching job in Scotland. He was only sixteen, which meant he was younger than some of his pupils. Being a scientific sort of person, he also experimented with speech—by tapping his throat while doing weird things with his mouth in the mirror at night to investigate vowel sounds.

In 1870, Aleck and his parents moved to Canada. He started his own speech school the next year, and the year after he was made a professor of Vocal Physiology at Boston but he had time for some top-secret inventing too.

A friend's father, Gardiner Hubbard, a wealthy businessmen in Boston, offered to back Aleck's research. So Aleck found an assistant called Watson and they set up a laboratory and got to work on the harmonic telegraph. And then, in 1875, Aleck accidentally invented half a telephone … all he had was a receiver!

---

tapping: strike lightly
weird: strange

To have a really satisfactory chat, you need to be able to talk as well as listen. So Aleck started work on a transmitter.

Even though Aleck didn't have a working phone yet, he thought he might manage it one day, so to be on the safe side he patented the idea, on February 14, 1876. In March 1876, Aleck said, "Mr Watson, come here, I want to see you" into his acid phone, and three rooms away, Watson heard him. The only thing was, the phone wasn't very reliable, very clear or very loud. So cunningly–he didn't use it as a telephone when he demonstrated it! Instead he impressed people with tricks like getting a little box to make a sound like an organ, a gimmick only partly based on his phone. Later on, Aleck demonstrated telephones in all sort of ways and places–including underwater …

He also went to England and showed his telephone to Queen Victoria. Aleck kept improving his phone and later formed the Bell Company.

The Bell Company was an amazing success, and the value of its shares rose and rose. Aleck had plenty of them, so he was soon very rich indeed, rich enough to retire and spend more time helping deaf people.

Aleck would never have a phone in his study. They were just too disturbing. On the whole, he preferred them when they were quiet. But from then on, they never were, except once, in 1922. All the phones in America were silent for one minute to mark his funeral.

---

transmitter: the part of a telephonic apparatus that converts sound waves or mechanical movements into corresponding electric waves or impulses
patented: an invention protected by law
gimmick: an ingenious device

Reading Comprehension

Answer the following questions.

1. What is Alexander Graham Bell famous for?
2. Why was Aleck keen on helping deaf people?
3. How did Aleck's grandfather, Aleck's father and Charles Wheatstone influence him?
4. How did Aleck get funding for his research?
5. Why did Aleck refuse to have a phone in his study?
6. What is the tone of this article? Does it convey a lot of information?

Vocabulary

Suffixes

> **Suffixes** are added to the end of a word to make a new word.

Add suffixes from the box to the words below to make new words.

Remember that in some cases you may need to drop the silent e while adding the suffix.

-al -ic -ity -hood -age -ian

person	________	break	________	athlete	________
child	________	guard	________	pack	________
idiot	________	adult	________	mystic	________
secure	________	logic	________		

Grammar

Adverbs

An **adverb** is a word that tells us more about a verb, an adjective, or another adverb.

Adverbs of time*:* These are used to show when something happens.

Adverbs of place*:* These are used to show where something happens.

Adverbs of manner*:* These are used to show how something happens.

Identify the adverbs of manner, time and place, and write them in the correct columns in the table below.

This morning we went outside to watch the sunrise.

The cadets marched forward briskly.

I hope I run fast in the race tomorrow.

Soon we will have to go inside.

Arun is going upstairs to get his calculator.

Yesterday Ann worked hard to finish knitting the sweater.

The gymnast did the routine perfectly.

Someday I hope to be able to write as neatly as you.

Adverbs of Time	Adverbs of Place	Adverbs of Manner

Adverbs of frequency describe how often an action takes place.

In the following sentences, underline the adverbs of frequency.

The new science teacher always gives us lots of homework.

We often go to Bangalore to visit my grandparents.

Anil and Nikhil rarely come to school on time.

Sometimes we play basketball in the games period.

My father never lets me go out by myself after 6 o'clock.

Rahim usually has a big party on his birthday.

Rahul always forgets to bring his books and is punished regularly.

Our neighbour is constantly complaining about the noise we make.

Spelling and Punctuation

Anagrams

An **anagram** is a type of word play, the result of rearranging the letters of a word or phrase to produce a new word or phrase, using all the original letters exactly once.

Can you work out these anagrams? Use the hints in the brackets if you need to.

clip in par (the most important person in school) ____________

rash preen (something you find in a pencil box) ____________

loft a lob (a sport) ____________

calms or so (where you study) ____________

an am rag (a word game!) ____________

Writing

Read the following phone conversation.

- Hello?
- Hello, may I speak to Mr Sharma?
- I'm sorry, he's not at home. May I know who's speaking, please?
- My name is Rajiv Khanna. Are you Mr Sharma's son?
- Yes, I'm his son, Vinay. Can I take a message?
- Will you ask your father to call me back? My number is 9056781234.
- I will. Goodbye!
- Goodbye!

Write a telephone message for Mr Sharma based on the conversation between Vinay and Rajiv Khanna.

Listening

Identify the household objects from the descriptions read by your teacher.

Speaking

With your partner, practice using could I and should I in conversations.

For example:

- Should I finish my work before the match?
- Could I go home early today?

Everyday English

You have read about the famous invention of Alexander Graham Bell. A telephone is a common instrument in almost every home.

Your telephone is out of order and you need to register your complaint in the Telephone Department.

You can practice the conversation using the following sentences:

- My phone is out of order.
- Since yesterday morning.
- The bell rings but I can't hear the other person speak.
- My address is 32-A Western Avenue.
- Thank you.

Activity

Crossword

Can you name the famous inventors who invented the things listed below?

ACROSS

1 Dynamite
4 Radio
5 TV
7 Petrol-powered car
8 Steam engine
9 Printing press

DOWN

2 World Wide Web
3 Sewing machine
6 Breakfast cornflakes

Read More

If you enjoyed reading this article, you can read the book from which it its taken: *Inventors and their Bright Ideas*. These are short biographies of different inventors. You can read other short biographies by Dr Michael Goldsmith, such as *Writers and their Tall Tales* and *Scientists and their Explosive Experiments*.

15 *Wilderness*

Roddy Doyle is an award-winning Irish author and screenwriter.

Johnny Griffin, nearly twelve, and his ten-year-old brother, Tom, lived in Dublin, with their parents. Their mother had booked an adventure holiday for them.

"Where?" asked Johnny.

"To a place with snow and reindeer and huskies and snowmobiles."

"Lapland in northern Finland."

Tom ran down the hall and got Johnny's atlas out of his schoolbag. Their mother showed them the route they'd be taking. Her finger went from Dublin, over the Irish Sea.

"We've to fly to Manchester first, then to Helsinki and then change planes and fly further north," she said.

They landed at Lapland and saw the signboard "Winter Safari". The boys opted for the safari on a dog sled.

Soon they gathered around the sled. There were no dogs attached to it yet. It was a simple wooden sled. There were two parallel runners, at the bottom, with a thin plate made of metal on each runner, to stand on. There was a brake bar across the back of the sled, just over the runners.

"Where are the reins?" asked Tom.

sled: a small vehicle consisting of a platform mounted on runners for travelling over snow or ice

"No reins," said Aki, their guide.

"Then how will we make the dogs go?" asked Johnny.

"You are very young," said Aki. "You'll go with Kalle."

Kalle was collecting the strips of leather, which would hold the huskies to the sleds, pulling the strips, making sure they wouldn't snap.

"The dogs will follow Kalle," said Aki.

Kalle showed them how to get the harness over a dog's head. He let them do it. And the dogs let them do it. The dogs licked their hands as they put the leather straps over their ears.

"The dogs licking their hands was a sign of friendliness," Aki told them. Tom patted the dog's head. The ears sprang back up. They were like little triangles stuck on top of his head.

The harness went around the dog's mouth, across the snout. The dogs let it happen; they didn't pull back or snarl. To show the boys how to hitch the husky dog to the sled, Kalle grabbed the collar of Johnny's dog and pulled the dog over the sled.

The sled was bigger than the others and would have eight dogs to pull it.

Tom liked the dogs' bushy tails, curled over their backs. The tails were a sign of how happy and excited the dogs were. They were going for a run.

Gradually, all the dogs were hitched to the sleds.

"Why can't we have a sled of our own?" asked Johnny.

"You are too light, not enough kilos on the brakes," replied Aki.

Kalle stood beside his sled, away from the brakes. The dogs wouldn't run away. Tom and Johnny sat beside each other, in front of Kalle, in a narrow hallow. The boys were nearly lying down. Kalle tucked the boys with a blanket as thick as a rug.

Suddenly, Johnny and Tom were moving fast. They started laughing. They were gliding over the snow, behind eight dogs. The dogs went straight out of the gate. The boys saw more snow than they'd ever seen before.

Johnny was so excited, he shouted, "Wilderness!"

And Tom joined in, like an echo.

"Wil-der-ness!"

---

harness: a combination of straps and bands used to control a horse or other animal

Reading Comprehension

Answer the following questions.

1. Where did Johnny and Tom live?
2. By what route did they travel to Lapland?
3. How did the boys choose to take the safari?
4. Why did the dogs lick their hands?
5. Why couldn't the boys be in a sled on their own?
6. What made Johnny excited?
7. What can you say about the characters of the two boys?

Vocabulary

Complete the following phrases with take, have or break.

________ a seat	________ a holiday	________ the silence
________ a taxi	________ a break	________ an ice cream
________ a promise		

Grammar

Clauses

> A **clause** is a group of words containing a subject and predicate that is part of a larger sentence.

Underline the clauses in the following sentences.

My father was reading a book which was about the Independence movement.

While we were waiting, Vivek told jokes that made us laugh.

Anand will be busy after his mother comes home.

Peter felt sick so he went to the school nurse.

Raja was playing badminton when he heard the news.
Mr Rao served coffee while Mrs Rao offered us biscuits.
When my uncle visits us, he brings us all presents.

A **sentence** can often contain more than one clause. When a clause in a sentence makes sense by itself it is a principal clause. When one clause depends on the other clause to make sense it is called a subordinate clause. A sentence can have more than one main clause, or it can have only one main clause with no subordinate clauses, or it may have a main clause and subordinate clause.

Identify the main clause and the subordinate clause.

Akanksha is wearing a new sweater, which is purple and yellow.
This is Mayank, who goes to my school.
Maria lives in Milan, which is in Italy.
Ramesh, who is my cousin, is very tall.
Mohan wore a shirt that had a big stain on it.
We all left the food, which was terrible.

Spelling and Punctuation

Direct speech

Rewrite the following as direct speech.

1. The old lady asked us if this was the way to the supermarket.
2. The children said that there was a problem with the plumbing.
3. We shouted at them to get off our land.
4. The monitor told the children to stand up.
5. Sheela exclaimed that she had found her purse.
6. Prakash asked Shikha if she was busy.

Writing

Write a review of any book you have read recently.

You should mention

- Book title
- Author name
- The character you liked best
- What went wrong
- How the problem was solved
- The funniest part
- The saddest part
- The sort of reader who would like the book
- Compare to a similar book you have read

Listening

Your teacher will read some questions about different countries and places. Can you answer them?

Speaking

Would you like to travel on a sleigh pulled by dogs? Ask your partner questions about the different ways of travelling.
Has your partner travelled by bus? By ship? By plane? What was it like?

Activity

Wil words

How many six-, seven-, eight-letter words can you make starting with wil-?

Read More

If you enjoyed this story, you could read the book from which it is taken: *Wilderness* by Roddy Doyle.

If you like reading adventure stories set among ice and wilderness, you can read books by Jack London.

16 Word Balloon

Sampurna Chattarji is an award-winning Indian poet.

I'd like to ride a word-balloon,
High up in the sky
Made of words like bandicoot
And caravanserai.

Or perhaps a word like
Gargantuan (that's big)
Or another one like excavate
Which really means to dig.

Sometimes I'll use lighter words
Like ethereal and fey,
Sometimes I'll use heavier ones
So I won't drift away–

Like conjugate and colossal
Like octahedral dome
Like ponderous and parliament
Like carious catacomb.

---

bandicoot: a rat-like marsupial
caravanserai: an inn
ethereal: light, airy
fey: having fairylike qualities
conjugate: to join together
colossal: huge
octahedral: eight-sided
ponderous: heavy
carious: decayed
catacomb: an underground cemetery

But the brightest ones will be
The best, the shiny happy words
Like scintillate and radiate
They'll fly like hummingbirds.

Don't ask me where I find them,
They're in the dictionary,
And back home I feed them all
To my pedigreed canary!

---

scintillate: to emit sparks
pedigreed: having established pure-bred ancestry
canary: small bird native to the Canary Islands

Reading Comprehension

Answer the following questions.

1. What do you think makes a word "light" or "heavy"?
2. How would the poet use words?
3. Can you think of some more "heavy" and "light" words?
4. How are hot-air balloons usually controlled?
5. Which poem in this book did you like the most? Why?

Vocabulary

Tick the correct word to complete the following.

(Say/Tell) those children to make less noise.

Ali (said/told) that he would come to visit us in October.

Remember to (say/tell) Vinita about the wedding.

My little brother likes me to (say/tell) him a story at bedtime.

The professor (said/told) us all about dinosaurs.

My mother (said/told) we could have a party after my brother's exams.

Use do/did/doing or make/made/making to complete the following sentences.

We are going to ____________________ dinner on Saturday.

Please __________________ your household chores first.

The crowd at the tennis match was _____________________ too much noise.

First __________ these sums and then _________________ a diagram.

I'm too tired to _________________ any work today.

When I was your age I ___________________ my own bed every morning.

Grammar

Personal and possessive pronouns

> **Possessive pronouns** are pronouns which show that something is owned by someone, while **personal pronouns** simply refer to a subject.

Determine whether the underlined words are personal or possessive pronouns.

Raghav and I went hiking last summer. _________________________

The desk in the front row is yours. _________________________

Nilanjana said they all wanted to watch the match. ____________________

Do you have Ankita's phone number? ____________________

These books are ours. ____________________

Jessica said that the piano was hers. ____________________

We are planning a holiday in Argentina. ____________________

Can she come to dinner at our house? ____________________

Can you see it? ____________________

France is a European country and Paris is its capital. ____________________

Relative pronouns

Relative pronouns connect a relative cause to a noun phrase. Words, such as whose, who, which and that, are often used as relative pronouns.

Underline the relative pronouns.

This is Ritesh, whose house I stayed at last year.

I know someone who studies in that school.

Did you like the dress that I wore to the party?

This is the house that Jack built.

We grow turnips, which are a kind of root vegetable.

Bhavneet, who is very tall, is good at basketball.

Reflexive pronouns

Reflexive pronouns refer back to the subject or object of the clause. Sometimes these pronouns are used for emphasis, to lay stress on the fact that we are referring to this person/thing and nobody else. In those cases they are called emphatic pronouns.

Underline the reflexive pronouns. Tick the box if they are being used as emphatic pronouns.

The principal herself came to see who was making the noise. ☐

My father cut himself while shaving this morning. ☐

After weeks of lying in bed, the patient was finally able to raise herself. ☐

The celebrity himself was polite, but his bodyguards were very rude. ☐

Shilpa does't understand that she herself is to blame. ☐

Can't you do anything by yourself? ☐

Spelling and Punctuation

Circle the errors in the following passage.

Hot-air ballooning as a adventure sports started in the year 1783, when two French brother Joseph Michel Montgolfier and Jacques Etienne Montgolfier, creats and sat aloft a 17.37-m high "fire balloon' from the courtyard of the Versailles palace. This massive ballon did not carry human passengers but a sheep a rooster and duck. The balloon lands safely at a distance of 3.2 km from the Versailles palace after a flight lasted eight minutes. In the same year, a darling person by the name of Jean Francois Pilatre de Rozier along with his companion Marquis d'Arlandes decided to travel in a hot air balloon. It became the first journey made by man from air, which was powered by steam/hot air. This historic event occurred in the beautiful city of Paris and the success of this flight in the nineteenth century had birth to the sport of hot-air ballooning.

Writing

Write a list of your five favourite words. Do you know what they mean?

How to Use a Dictionary

A dictionary is a book that lists the words of a language and gives their meanings.
People use a dictionary to find the meaning and the correct spelling of a word.
A dictionary also has some details about words such as their function or part of speech, their pronunciation, as well as origins or roots.
Other useful information, such as English to metric conversion tables, maps, explanations of common symbols, can be found in a dictionary.
There are separate dictionaries for languages, rhymes, slangs, idioms, geographical entries and medical terms.

*Let's start by locating the word **start**.*

Remember all words in a dictionary are listed in alphabetical order. This means that all the words beginning with the letter A are in the front and words beginning with the letter Z are in the back of the dictionary.

1. Open the dictionary so that it lies flat on the table before you.

2. Go to the pages that have words starting with the letter S. Scan through the words that are close to the first or first two letters of the word.

3. Notice the guide words at the top of each page. These words will guide you to the right page. The first guide word is the first word on a page, and the second guide word is the last word on the page. You can find your word between the two guide words.

4. You will now see all the words beginning with the letters st. Move to the third letter and keep moving down till you find the word start.

   Start (stärt) v. 1. to begin to do, be or happen. 2. begin to operate. 3. cause to happen or operate. n. 1. an act of beginning or the point at which something begins. 2. an advantage given at the beginning of a race. Phrases for a start in the first place. Start out (or up), begin a project or business. To start with as the first thing to be taken into account.

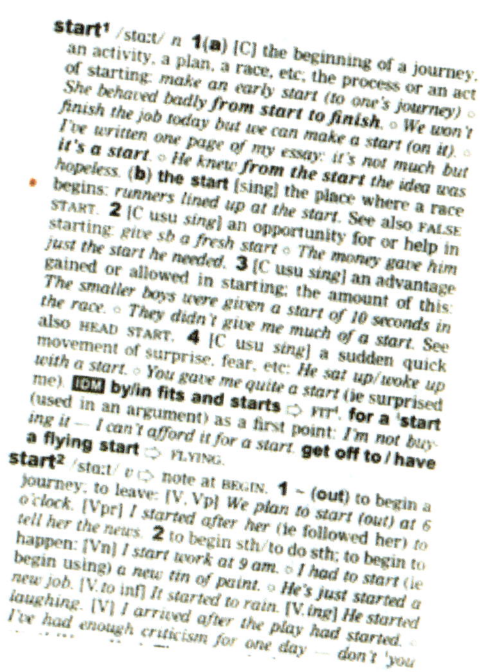

start¹ /stɑːt/ *n* **1(a)** [C] the beginning of a journey, an activity, a plan, a race, etc; the process or an act of starting: *make an early start (to one's journey)* ◦ *She behaved badly **from start to finish**.* ◦ *We won't finish the job today but we can make a start (on it).* ◦ *I've written one page of my essay: it's not much but **it's a start**.* ◦ *He knew **from the start** the idea was hopeless.* **(b) the start** [sing] the place where a race begins: *runners lined up at the start.* See also FALSE START. **2** [C usu sing] an opportunity for or help in starting: *give sb a fresh start* ◦ *The money gave him just the start he needed.* **3** [C usu sing] an advantage gained or allowed in starting; the amount of this: *The smaller boys were given a start of 10 seconds in the race.* ◦ *They didn't give me much of a start.* See also HEAD START. **4** [C usu sing] a sudden quick movement of surprise, fear, etc: *He sat up/woke up with a start.* ◦ *You gave me quite a start* (ie surprised me). IDM **by/in fits and starts** ⇨ FIT⁴. **for a 'start** (used in an argument) as a first point: *I'm not buying it — I can't afford it for a start.* **get off to / have a flying start** ⇨ FLYING.
start² /stɑːt/ *v* ⇨ note at BEGIN. **1** ~ **(out)** to begin a journey; to leave: [V, Vp] *We plan to start (out) at 6 o'clock.* [Vpr] *I started after her* (ie followed her) *to tell her the news.* **2** to begin sth/to do sth; to begin to happen: [Vn] *I start work at 9 am.* ◦ *I had to start* (ie begin using) *a new tin of paint.* ◦ *He's just started a new job.* [V.to inf] *It started to rain.* [V.ing] *He started laughing.* [V] *I arrived after the play had started.* ◦ *I've had enough criticism for one day — don't 'you*

If you can't seem to locate your word, make sure you are spelling the word right. You will not find the word honest under the o words.

Try using the word in a sentence. If it's difficult to spell, write it a few times to remember it.

How to Use a Thesaurus

A thesaurus is a book containing lists of words that have the same, similar or a related meaning. Some thesauri may also contain antonyms, wordlists and other interesting features. A thesaurus is a resource that will help you avoid repeating a word while writing. It helps you find a word for an idea you have in mind.

You can use a thesaurus to increase your vocabulary.

Most thesauri, like dictionaries, have words arranged in alphabetical order—starting with the letter A and ending with the letter Z.

The words in a thesaurus are followed immediately by a short list of synonyms.

A word may have many words as synonyms. Be careful in choosing the word with the correct contextual meaning.

For example:
Start: approach, begin, commence, embark, enter, get off, inaugurate, initiate, institute, launch, lead off, open, set about, set out, set to, take on, take up, undertake

stanza *n* verse, canto, strophe, stave, refrain, strain ➡ **poem**

star 1. *n* sun
2. *n* ➡ **celebrity, actor**

stare *vb* gaze, peer, gape, ogle, gawk ➡ **look**

start 1. *vb* begin, commence, initiate, cause, activate, launch, originate, stem, inaugurate, introduce, innovate, open, trigger, touch off, spark ➡ **continue** ⇨ ***finish, stop***
2. *n* ➡ **beginning**
3. *vb* ➡ **jump**

state 1. *n* condition, circumstance, situation, status, stage, phase ➡ **grade**
2. *n* territory, province, dominion, commonwealth ➡ **country, colony, zone**
3. *vb* ➡ **mention, say, tell**

stationary *adj* fixed, immobile, permanent, motionless, steady, stable, still, stock-still, inert, stagnant ⇨ ***portable***

statue *n* sculpture, statuette, figure, figurine, bust, bronze, likeness, image, effigy, idol, statuary ➡ **monument**

steal 1. *vb* rob, swipe, snatch, shoplift, purloin, embezzle, burglarize, rifle, poach, pinch, pilfer, pocket, plagiarize, pirate, filch ➡ **take, seize; pillage**
2. *vb* ➡ **sneak**
3. *n* ➡ **bargain**

steep 1. *adj* sheer, abrupt, precipitous, sharp, perpendicular, vertical, uphill
2. *vb* ➡ **wet**

step 1. *n* footstep, stride, pace, tread, footfall
2. *n* ➡ **gait**
3. *n* ➡ **act**
4. *n* rung, tread, stair ➡ **grade**
5. *vb* ➡ **walk, dance**

stereotype 1. *n* convention, generalization, categorization, characterization ➡ **cliché**
2. *vb* categorize, pigeonhole, characterize, label, generalize

Listening texts

Lesson 1

1. Dantes liked being in the Chateau d'If.
2. Dantes' friend Faria was dead.
3. The bearers threw Dantes into the sea.
4. The Chateau d'If had a graveyard next to it.
5. This story is set in India.

Lesson 2

1. bread, french fries, biscuits, cakes, muffins.
2. pencil, pen, ruler, crayon, quill.
3. elbow, mouth, eyes, nose, tongue.
4. shout, whisper, jump, scream, yellow.

Lesson 3

1. This animal eats leaves from trees. It has a very long neck.
2. Often wrongly called a bear, this small cuddly animal lives in trees and is native to Australia.
3. This animal is covered with black and white stripes. It has four hooves, like a horse.
4. This animal comes from Australia. It moves by jumping, and has a pouch in front to carry its baby.
5. This animal comes from China. It eats leaves and bamboo shoots. It is covered in black and white fur.

Lesson 4

Three children went for a walk by the river in Norway. There was no bridge. They did not have a boat or raft or any material to build one. No one could swim. How did they get across?

Answer: The river was frozen.

Lesson 5

1. knowledge
2. biting
3. written
4. thought
5. honesty
6. kitchen

Lesson 6

1. Who is the president of India?
2. What is the capital of Pakistan?
3. Which country won the last cricket World Cup?
4. How many states are there in India?
5. Who is the president of the USA?
6. Who is the prime minister of India?

Lesson 7

Last week, when my mother and I had gone shopping, my father lost his spectacles. He could not find them anywhere. They were not on his desk. They were not in the kitchen or the bathroom. They were not on the dining table. He even checked the garden, but the spectacles were nowhere to be found. He was very upset about losing them because now he couldn't read the newspaper.

When he heard us ring the doorbell he quickly opened the door. He said 'I have lost my spectacles! Will you help me find them?'

We stared at him for a moment. Then we both burst out laughing.

Lesson 9

tailor

chef

Race-car driver

doctor

movie director

tennis player

Lesson 10

A father and his son were travelling by train. Unfortunately, there was a train crash. In the accident, the father was killed and the son was badly wounded.

The son was taken to hospital immediately so that he could be operated upon. But on seeing the boy the surgeon turned pale and said, 'I cannot do this operation. That boy is my son.'

Answer: The surgeon is the mother.

Lesson 11

While horse riding Usha uses the reins to control the horse.

In August it rains all the time and we can't go out to play.

In the mornings we heard the loud peal of the church bell.

The clown slipped on a banana peel and fell over.

You should learn to sew buttons onto your shirt by yourself.

I finished my homework early so that I could go out in the evening.

The match was cancelled due to bad weather conditions.

I don't know whether my brother will be coming today or tomorrow.

Lesson 13

1. My father was feeling a little under the weather so he didn't go to work today.
2. Don't worry about the Maths Olympiad; we've got it in the bag!
3. Bhavna has been in this profession for a long time and knows the ropes.
4. Amir hated the new movie and Maryam loved it, but I'm on the fence.
5. We almost got away with the prank, but the teacher smelt a rat.

Lesson 14

1. It runs on electricity. We use it to take the wrinkles out of our clothes.
2. It broadcasts pictures and sounds. It has a screen.
3. It broadcasts sounds but not pictures. It can be tuned to different stations.
4. It is found in the bathroom. It is used to heat water.
5. It is used in the kitchen. It keeps food cool and fresh.

Lesson 15

1. What is the capital of England?
2. What is the capital of Egypt?
3. What is the capital of Pakistan?
4. Where is Santa Claus said to come from?
5. Where is the river Nile?
6. What did Christopher Columbus discover?

Evaluation Table

Name: ____________________

Class: __________

Title	Comprehension		Vocabulary	Spelling and Punctuation	Grammar
	Reading for facts	Making inferences			
1. The Cemetery of the Chateau d'If					
2. Yudhishtir the Just					
3. What's Eating You?					
4. Trees					
5. After Twenty Years					
6. I'm Only a Child					
7. Don't Do As I Say					
8. He Wishes for the Cloths of Heaven					
9. All About Stars					
10. In the Fog					
11. The Boy Who Could Not Finish A					
12. Three Characters					
13. Bani Chatterjee and the Burden of Expectation					
14. Alexander Graham Bell					
15. Wilderness					
16. Word Balloon					

Writing			Speaking		Listening
Organisation of ideas	Making connections	Expression	Confdence	Fluency	

Acknowledgements

The publishers would like to thank the following for permission to use copyrighted material:

Anushka Ravishankar for 'Three Characters'; Baaraan Ijlaal for the illustrations for 'Yudhishtir the Just' and 'Don't Do As I Say'; Blake Education for the activities Word Game, Shrinking Words, Word Change, Word Origins, Mystery Word, Man Words, Proverbs and Group of Three from *Brainteasers, Puzzles and Games Level 3* (Scholastic India: 2008); Nury Vittachi for 'The Boy Who Could Not Finish A' from *Funny Stories* (Scholastic India: 2007); Priya Kuriyan for the illustrations of 'The Boy Who Could Not Finish A', 'Three Characters' and 'Bani Chatterjee and the Burden of Expectation'; Samit Basu for 'Bani Chatterjee and the Burden of Expectation' from *Be Witched* (Scholastic India: 2008); Sampurna Chattarji for 'Word Balloon'; Scholastic Children's Books UK for 'What's Eating You?' from Horrible Science: Nasty Nature by Nick Arnold (Scholastic UK: 1997) and the accompanying illustrations by Tony de Saulles; 'Alexander Graham Bell' from *Dead Famous: Inventors and Their Bright Ideas* by Dr Mike Goldsmith (Scholastic UK: 2002) and the accompanying illustrations by Clive Goddard; and 'Wilderness' from *Wilderness* by Roddy Doyle (Scholastic UK: 2007) and the accompanying illustration by Brad Wrobleski; Scholastic Inc. for 'After Twenty Years' from *Mystery Plays* by Tom Conkin (Scholastic Inc: 2007); and 'All About Stars' from *Do Stars Have Points?* by Melvin and Gilda Berger (Scholastic Inc: 1998) and the accompanying illustrations by Vincent di Fate; Shahrukh Hussain for 'Don't Do As I Say' from *The Wisdom of Mulla Nasruddin* (Scholastic India: 2006); Subrata Guha for 'Yudhishtir the Just' from *Mahabharata: The War* by Soma Guha (Scholastic India: 2007); Vivekananda Roy Ghatak for the illustrations for 'Word Balloon'; Zainab Tambawalla for the illustrations for 'Into the Fog'.

While every attempt has been made to trace copyright holders for the text, illustrations and photographs, this has not been possible in all cases. Any omissions brought to our attention will be rectified in future editions.